The
KINDNESS
of GOD

David Smith has once again provided a series of penetrating essays that provoke us to think freshly not only about the missiological challenges out there – Islam, globalisation, urban growth, the post-Christian West – but also the challenges at home that we so easily neglect – a church shaped by materialism, a gospel distorted by secular culture, a proclamation of the cross without the experience of its weakness and power. In this troubled world, he urges us to rediscover the fullness of the gospel, to engage anew with Paul's teaching to the urban poor of Rome, and to listen to the voices of compassion from the underside of globalisation. We stand at the cusp of an exciting new era of church growth and mission, and this book provokes reflection on the hope which flows from the kindness of God. It is an urgent, prophetic and compassionate book that is rooted in our broken world but lifts our eyes to see God's purposes for his global church.

Jonathan Lamb, Director, Langham Preaching

ivp

The
KINDNESS
of GOD

Christian witness in
our troubled world

DAVID W. SMITH
Foreword by Lamin Sanneh

INTER-VARSITY PRESS
Norton Street, Nottingham NG7 3HR, England
Email: ivp@ivpbooks.com
Website: www.ivpbooks.com

First published 2013

British Library Cataloguing in Publication Data
A catalogue record for this book is available from the British Library.

ISBN: 978–1–84474–649–1

Set in Dante 12/15pt
Typeset in Great Britain by CRB Associates, Potterhanworth, Lincolnshire
Printed and bound in Great Britain by Ashford Colour Press Ltd.

Inter-Varsity Press publishes Christian books that are true to the Bible and that communicate the gospel, develop discipleship and strengthen the church for its mission in the world.

Inter-Varsity Press is closely linked with the Universities and Colleges Christian Fellowship, a student movement connecting Christian Unions in universities and colleges throughout Great Britain, and a member movement of the International Fellowship of Evangelical Students. Website: www.uccf.org.uk.

Contents

Foreword   7
Introduction   12

Part 1: Mission in a troubled world
1. From Edinburgh, 1910, to Jos, 2012   21
2. Critical issues concerning the gospel and culture   37
3. Mission, violence and suffering   55
4. Translating the gospel for the globalized world
    of the twenty-first century   76

**Part 2: Releasing the message of the Bible
for a divided church and a troubled world**
5. The Bible and globalization: critical reflections
    on biblical hermeneutics   95
6. The letter to the Romans and mission in a
    troubled, urban world   120

Conclusion: witness to – and in – the kindness
of God   151

For Sammy and Laurie
who have brought a new kind of joy into
the lives of their grandparents, and
teach us what the kingdom of God really means

(Matthew 19:13–15)

Foreword

This book is personal testimony, set in the context of the ferment and unrest evident in much of the world in recent times, and is dedicated to looking for hope and courage against the odds. Where is the kindness of God in all this? Indeed, what is the kindness of God in a world we all share, even if we share it unevenly? What are the implications for Christianity and for Christians in the current global resurgence of the religion? The answers to these questions are intimately connected to the contemporary political ferment in Islam and the extent to which that implicates Christian life and witness, as David Smith points out in his reflections.

Beginning with the Protestant ecumenical missionary conference in Edinburgh in 1910, strategists began pondering the challenge confronting the church in the modern era. The rapid changes in Europe were creating a new situation in which Europe's Christian ties were being loosened, while at the same time Christianity was poised to strike out on its post-Western errand without the compromise and burden of empire. It confronted the strategists with two challenges, the first having to do with the meaning of the Christian heritage in a post-Christian West, and the second with the Christian awakening in the religion's post-Western phase. Many perceptive observers see a promising connection between these two developments: the significance of the gospel in a post-Christian West can only be enhanced by evidence of the movements of conversion occurring in the post-Western world. The parameters of mission have now been expanded to embrace a much richer and more challenging understanding of commitment and witness than the old European paradigms. The world God so loved, and for which Christ died, transcends and challenges all artificial and natural boundaries – that has always been true. But that truth is now presented to us from a new radical angle concerning 'the kindness of God'. This is different from how state boundaries are being levelled down and dismantled by global forces for the exploitation and accumulation of commodities and market share, for that only redraws the boundaries in favour of capital and advantage. By contrast, the contours of the worldwide Christian movement make ample room for new forms of mission and discipleship that spare neither the entitlements of a post-Christian West nor the defensiveness of a post-Western world. Those who share faith in Christ share that in a converging world that is designed in such a way that nothing can separate us from one another, thanks to the love of God in Christ. The ubiquity of the global market in a flat world is not the same as the solicitude of the reconciled fellowship of God's redeeming work in Christ.

The movements of conversion in post-colonial societies are evidence of hidden currents that, meanwhile, have been stirring the waters of the coming global cultural shift that has not spared the West. That was the assessment of Samuel Huntington in his widely acclaimed book, *The Clash of Civilizations and the Remaking of World Order*. The book tempered the claims of secular ascendancy by arguing that new cultural fault lines are emerging to threaten global stability. While the champions of secularization are confident that the collapse of Soviet communism has left Western liberal democracy in uncontested control of the field, Huntington argues that such confidence is misplaced, because there are recrudescent ideologies that contest Western dominance, including divergent and hostile religious traditions. Muslims, Chinese and Indians, Huntington notes, are not all suddenly going to fall into line behind Western liberalism. 'The more fundamental divisions of humanity in terms of ethnicity, religions, and civilizations remain and spawn new conflicts'.[1]

The secularized world as the object and subject of Christian engagement is far from being an innocent undertaking. As Arthur Koestler predicted in the decade before Vatican II, the geometrical design of the evolution of communication and understanding would reach the point of near-saturation, bringing about instant global interconnectedness, but without that making for moral cohesiveness and the awareness of a unified humanity. People would possess the power and means of accessing information and knowledge without the capacity for charity and inter-personal trust. The advent of virtual communication that was only vaguely glimpsed at the time would not remove intercultural impediments. 'The stupendous amplification of vision and hearing caused a rapid deterioration of the intellectual and moral content of communication . . . Our diagrams show an unprecedented increase in the range and power of the species' sensory and motor organs coincident with a marked deterioration of the integrative functions which determine spiritual maturity and social ethics.' The implication is that the challenge of the modern age is to persuade humankind to do more than 'to acquiesce in its own demotion'. Without a coherent ethical framework, the threat to human prospering and to the fabric of the common good would accelerate, spreading conflict and intolerance. Citing Cicely Wedgwood, Koestler described how in another instance the results of the dismantling of the spiritual centrepiece of

---

1. Samuel P. Huntington, *The Clash of Civilizations and the Remaking of World Order* (New York: Simon and Schuster, 1997), pp. 66–67.

religion in the Thirty Years War created a vacuum at the heart of Europe, requiring a new emotional charge to fill the place of spiritual conviction. The new imperatives of human destiny took down the altars to leave people with the illusion of a vacuous sense of exhilaration but, occupying a lower order than men and women, without being able to offer any inspiration for faith and guidance for conscience. The shift from 'destiny from above' to 'destiny from below' shuts us into the besetting monotony of our own ideologies and inventions.

The issues that in equal measure have galvanized and jostled knowledgeable observers like Koestler and Huntington concern religion, or more precisely, the appeal to new assertive forms of religious activism and identity. In the West and beyond the issue of identity in terms of self-avowal and belonging, according to Huntington, is fundamentally a religious question, and for people caught in the currents of change and challenge, 'religion provides compelling answers, and religious groups provide small social communities [able] to replace those lost through urbanization'.[2] In that sense secularization acts as a mediation of religion, suggesting that neither a post-Christian West nor the world of traditional society is immune to outbreaks of religious assertiveness. It calls for the renewal of theistic faith and new forms of religious mobilization.

In this situation being a Christian demands attention to matters more than those of the individual as an autonomous unit shut up to his or her own thoughts, feelings, emotions and dispositions. In place of the old critique of primal cultures that sees them as inferior to the advanced technological cultures of Europe, Smith looks for commitment to values and practices that promote interfaith understanding as well as 'social harmony and human well-being'. The conclusion is

2. Huntington, *Clash of Civilizations*, p. 97.

inescapable that faithful Christian engagement with the world and with others is bound to lead to deeper truth about the gospel and God's work in the world.

The new development facing us in the post-Christian West and in a post-Western world calls for a fresh interpretation of the religious and ethical injunctions of apostolic faith. There is the call, on one side, of cutting loose the old moorings of conquest and domination, and, on the other, abandoning ethnic and cultural defensiveness. The gospel is about the crossing of boundaries, about an intercultural and inter-personal penetration that connects and sustains. It blurs the boundary between missionary transmission and local reception. The 'sending' of the gospel is effected and vindi-cated in the receiving of it. The sending bears fruit only in the receiving, which warrants a dynamic, unfolding understand-ing of mission and of belonging. St Bonaventura has rightly noted that the nature of God is as a circle of which the centre is everywhere and the circumference nowhere, suggesting a commodious theocentric vision of the faith community.

David Smith places his reflections on theology in the frame of a changing world, and his attentiveness to world events enables him to bring his reflections to life. The ground of his theological undertaking is the solid one of lived experi-ence, with all its uncertainties and challenges. The book abounds with questions forced upon us by the exigencies of life, reminding us of our inescapable duty and obligation to live and witness to the one sovereign God in a world organized and ruled by others. That reality remains a common challenge between the advanced secular West and the expanding frontiers of the post-Western resurgence.

Lamin Sanneh
Yale Divinity School, New Haven, Connecticut, USA

Introduction

The context within which the studies which make up the bulk of this book came to birth requires some explanation. Early in 2012 I received an invitation to speak on the topic of 'Mission in a Troubled World' at a conference of African theological educators to be held later that year at the Theological College of Northern Nigeria (TCNN) in the city of Jos. I was familiar both with this city and with the college; indeed, some years earlier I had spoken at a similar conference held there and had made other visits to teach both at TCNN and at the Jos Evangelical Theological Seminary (JETS). That being so, I understood very well the significance of the proposed title for this conference; the city of Jos, situated on a beautiful plateau from which the state in which it is located takes its name, had become a deeply divided and troubled community. The widely promoted image of Jos as 'The Home of Peace and Tourism' had become a hollow political slogan, undermined by increasingly frequent and ever more violent outbursts of inter-communal and inter-religious conflict. On a previous visit my wife and I had found ourselves very close to these troubles, confined to our residence for days by a twenty-four-hour curfew, while gunfire could be heard night and day beyond the walls of the guest house in which we were staying. The invitation to return to Jos arrived as trouble was erupting again and the British Foreign Office was once more advising its citizens to undertake travel to the Nigerian Plateau only if it could be classified as 'essential'.

Was my journey between the Nigerian capital Abuja and the troubled city of Jos essential? I learned that the deteriorating security situation had led American participants expected at the conference to withdraw from involvement, and there were reports of long-term Western residents in Jos packing up and departing. A church I knew well was targeted by a car bomber as the congregation gathered for Sunday worship and it was said that TCNN was itself on an intercepted hit-list drawn up by the radical Islamist group, Boko Harum. A new question surfaced: would theological teachers from other parts of Nigeria now attend the planned conference? Previous events had attracted significant numbers from all parts of the country, but would people want to travel to Jos in these present circumstances? The reasons for *not* going to Nigeria seemed to be piling up.

In truth there was never any real doubt but that I would fly to Nigeria and then take the journey up to Jos for this conference. In my mind attendance at this event was indeed absolutely essential. In the first place, how could I not identify with the friends and colleagues, both Nigerian and expatriate, whose work as theological educators on the fault line between Christianity and Islam in Africa I had so long admired? If they were convinced that the planned conference should go ahead I knew that this judgment was to be trusted. Indeed, not only were they so convinced, but it was clear they felt strongly that this was precisely the time and place when some serious critical reflection on mission was urgently required. I had previously described my colleagues in Jos as people 'whose commitment to discovering the way of Christ in a context characterized by deep religious and ethnic divisions' demonstrated 'a shining example of what it really means to do Christian theology in the cutting-edge situations of a pluralist world today'.[1] More than a decade later this judgment appeared to be more than ever true and consequently, I felt privileged to be invited to visit my friends and engage with them in wrestling with some of the most urgent and difficult issues facing Christianity in a globalized world.

But there was a second reason to regard my journey as 'essential'. The official advice to avoid anything other than essential travel, together with the understandable concerns of friends and family, could not be ignored, but a culture in which risks are always avoided and personal safety becomes the primary motivation for taking decisions hardly fits with the radical demands of discipleship in the New Testament. I remembered my first entry into Africa, which involved a night drive across a country devastated by civil war, on shattered roads which, my travelling companions informed me, were infested by armed robbers. For the first time in my life I understood Paul's boasting in his troubles, especially his claim to have been 'in danger from bandits . . . in danger in the city, in danger in the country . . . ' (2 Cor. 11:26), and his conclusion that his weaknesses and hardships were the vehicle for God's strength and grace: 'For when I am weak, then I am strong' (2 Cor. 12:10). I am not naturally a brave person and I certainly do not have a 'martyr complex', but that journey to Jos for the conference with African

1. David W. Smith, *Against the Stream: Christianity and Mission in an Age of Globalization* (Leicester: IVP, 2003), p. 8.

brothers and sisters wrestling with the challenge of mission in the midst of violence and deepening social divisions, seemed to me to be 'essential' from the perspective of obedience to Christ as my Lord. When the advice of one's government comes into conflict with the imperatives of the gospel, the outcome for anyone who takes the way of the crucified Messiah seriously cannot be in doubt.

Finally, there was a third factor which made it 'essential' for me to be present in Jos. The topic of 'Mission in a Troubled World' was close to a whole raft of issues which have been of central importance in my life and work for a long time, so the opportunity to spend time with colleagues whose lives are lived in contexts shaped by the forces of post-colonialism, globalization and constant interaction with other religious traditions was likely to be the source of enrichment and deepening understanding. While I felt that I had something to contribute to the discussions, I wanted to listen to people whose lives are lived in Jos, or further north where they are part of an embattled minority in strongly Muslim areas. For these friends and colleagues the struggle with the challenges of Christian discipleship takes place amid the tensions, un-certainties and fears generated in a context of deepening social and religious divisions. As will become clear at the end of this book, this expectation of personal enrichment and enhanced knowledge was to be wonderfully fulfilled.

The material contained in the first four chapters of this book consists of the lectures which I offered to the Jos confer-ence in May 2012. They are printed substantially as delivered then, with only minor alterations and the provision of some additional references to sources. The briefer second part of the book contains two studies concerning the use of the Bible in the shaping of the Christian understanding of mission. The first of these looks at the way in which Scripture was used to justify the political and economic expansion of European power at the dawn of the modern world and explores some crucial questions with regard to hermeneutics in our globalized context today. This began life as a paper for the Fellowship of Bible Agencies International (FOBAI) conference in Edinburgh in April 2011, and I must thank Dr Fergus MacDonald who invited me to prepare this material for FOBAI, and then generously requested that it be repeated at a conference of ministers of the Free Church of Scotland in Edinburgh in January 2012. The feedback and discussion resulting from this paper on both occasions was much appreciated and has contributed considerably to its substantial revision for publication here. The penultimate chapter in this book argues that mission in our troubled world demands both a new hermeneutic and a revised theology of mission, within which the letter of Paul to the Romans will play a fundamentally significant role. A rather different version of this was shared with participants to an interdisciplinary consultation on urbanization held at International Christian College in Glasgow in June 2012 and, once again, I am deeply grateful for the interaction with colleagues which took place then.

It is Paul's striking use of the phrase 'the kindness of God' in a passage in Romans (11:22) in which he wrestles with the ambiguities of history and the rise and fall of nations which I have taken as the title for this book. Having explained the tragic situation of his own Jewish people in terms of their experience of the divine 'sternness', the apostle to the Gentiles warns non-Jewish believers in the imperial city of Rome to beware of arrogance, counselling them to 'be afraid' that the appearance of the same sort of spiritual pride which led to the downfall of biblical Israel, will also be their undoing. In the deeply troubled times described in this book, this disturbing text speaks in powerful ways to Christians through-out our world, summoning a world church to prioritize what really matters and to discover its unity in the service of the Christ whose life and death displayed in human form precisely the kindness of God. And this serves to underline the fact that, although most of these studies had their origin in relation to the specific African situation described above, *the issues under discussion here are of absolutely fundamental importance to Christian believers throughout our one world today.*

I must express my gratitude to Dr Tersur Aben, Provost of the Theological College of Northern Nigeria, and to Dr Timothy Palmer, for their invitation to speak at the Jos confer-ence. Mark and Isabelle Hopkins, long-time members of staff at TCNN, provided, not for the first time, extremely generous hospitality and were once again stimulating and encouraging conversation partners. The list of people with whom I was privileged to engage in conversation on the topic of these lectures is too long to mention each individual, but I must express my thanks to all who participated in the conference for their fellowship, feedback, and above all, the examples of their devoted and faithful witness in difficult and challenging circumstances. I must mention Musa and Pamela Gaiya who welcomed me to their home and transported me back to Abuja, and Dr Paul Baillie of Mission Africa, who assisted me in various ways, offered stimulating comments on my material, and kept me amused with his unique brand of self-deprecating humour.

The photographs which illustrate this book have been supplied from various sources and the help of the following people is gratefully acknowledged: Paul Weston, Ken Osborne, Archivist at the Church Mission Society, Hugh Gaffney of the Keir Hardie Society, and the staff at the WCC archives in Geneva.

Sincere thanks are due to colleagues at Inter-Varsity Press who have supported this project from its inception, affirmed the importance of the issues I seek to address, and allowed me liberty to attempt to think new thoughts concerning the practice of mission today. I have been especially privileged to work once again with Phil Duce whose editorial skills and theological acumen combine to provide authors with an unrivalled level of help and encouragement.

Finally, I am profoundly grateful to Professor Lamin Sanneh who agreed to read this manuscript and has written a generous foreword. I share with him a huge debt to Professor Andrew Walls (as will be evident in the citations of his works which pepper the following pages); Lamin Sanneh is continuing and extending that same tradition of careful scholarship in ways that have made him one of the most distinguished and important scholars working in the field of mission studies today. More than that, his own pilgrimage provides an inspiring and deeply challenging perspective on all the issues addressed in the following pages, while presenting a living testimony to 'the kindness of God'.[2] It is humbling that he should be willing to comment on this present book.

David Smith
December, 2012

---

2. Lamin Sanneh, *Summoned From The Margin: Homecoming of an African* (Grand Rapids: Eerdmans, 2012).

PART 1:
MISSION IN A
TROUBLED WORLD

From Edinburgh, 1910, to Jos, 2012

In December 1996 the British missionary theologian Lesslie
Newbigin stood up to address a World Council of Churches'
conference at Salvador de Bahia in Brazil. It was to be his final
public message; he was now eighty-seven years of age and
had lost his sight. Despite his reputation as one of the most
prophetic of contemporary missionary thinkers, the organ-
izers of the conference had assumed that he would be unable
to contribute much of significance and so had allotted him
only a brief slot between two major sessions. However,
Newbigin failed to keep to the script. When he ran over time
the chairman handed him a note saying, 'Your time is up!'.
Newbigin's blindness meant that he was unable to read the
message and, to the delight of his audience, he simply carried
on speaking! What Lesslie Newbigin said on that occasion has
been called his 'swan song' on the ecumenical stage and it
provides the starting point for the reflections I wish to offer
here on the subject of 'mission in a troubled world'.

Newbigin repeated some of the themes which he had
developed during the extraordinarily fruitful final decades of

his life when, having returned from cross-cultural missionary service in India, he directed his attention toward the missionary challenge presented by the modern Western world. Describing this as the most urgent and difficult missionary frontier at the present time, he spoke with undiminished passion and clarity:

> The most powerful and pervasive of all the cultures of the world at this present time is that one which has been developed in Europe in the past two or three hundred years and which has created a global unity based on the science, the technology, and the ideology of the free market.[1]

Newbigin went on to claim that the only serious challenge to the scientific, secular culture emanating from the Western world is that offered by Islam, which 'with a courage that should put us Christians to shame, is openly challenging the claim that the free market and all its ideology is what rules the world'. Looking ahead into the third millennium, Newbigin concluded with these words, which will form the basis of my reflections in this and later chapters:

> And it seems to me that in the century that lies ahead of us these are the three major factors which will compete for the

1. Lesslie Newbigin, *Signs Amid the Rubble: The Purposes of God in Human History*, ed. Geoffrey Wainwright (Grand Rapids: Eerdmans, 2003), p. 117. Newbigin first addressed the challenge of mission to the contemporary Western world in *The Other Side of 1984: Questions for the Churches* (Geneva: WCC, 1983), a small book which created a great stir. The best way of accessing his subsequent work is through *Lesslie Newbigin: Missionary Theologian. A Reader*, ed. Paul Weston (London: SPCK, 2006).

allegiance of the human family: *the gospel, the free market, and Islam* . . . As to Islam: while the other great world faiths are deeply significant and worthy of respect, none of them makes the same claim for universal allegiance. As to the free market: the crucial question is going to be whether the Christian church can recover its confidence in the gospel in order to be able to challenge the tremendous power of this ideology which now rules over us.[2]

Lesslie Newbigin

What is striking in this statement is that while the missionary frontier with Islam is recognized as an obvious priority, Newbigin did not regard it as the supreme challenge of our times. That, he believed, was constituted by modern, Western

---

2. Newbigin, *Signs Amid the Rubble*, pp. 119–120, emphasis added.

culture which, through the process of globalization, had come to dominate every part of the earth. In Newbigin's view, the ideology of the free market involves something far more powerful and sinister than a neutral economic theory; it constitutes a *worldview* which defines people in terms of what they possess and consume. Behind the slogans of 'civilization', 'progress' and 'development', Lesslie Newbigin detected the presence of hideous forms of idolatry which demand exposure, challenge and repudiation by people who confess Jesus Christ as Lord. My purpose in what follows is to use Newbigin's analysis of the contemporary historical and cultural context to explore what might be involved in the practice of Christian mission in the 'troubled world' of the early twenty-first century.

Mission and Western civilization

Just over one hundred years ago, on Monday 14 June 1910 to be precise, the World Missionary Conference opened in the city of Edinburgh, Scotland. As many recent studies have shown, this was a key event in the history of Western missions and it represented the high watermark of the modern missionary movement. The dominant mood among the delegates was one of confidence in the success of the work of world evangelization, expressed in the famous slogan, 'The evangelization of the world in this generation'. Brian Stanley has described the prevailing atmosphere at the time as one of 'boundless optimism and unsullied confidence in the ideological and financial power of western Christendom'.[3] And yet, it is possible to detect signs that not far beneath the

---

3. Brian Stanley, *The World Missionary Conference, Edinburgh 1910* (Grand Rapids: Eerdmans, 2009), p. 16.

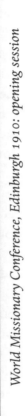

World Missionary Conference, Edinburgh 1910: opening session

surface of this public confidence, which sometimes bordered on triumphalism, there lurked a growing fear that the future might be far more uncertain than the dominant rhetoric suggested. For example, the report of the commission on 'Carrying the Gospel to all the Non-Christian World', while viewing the whole world as 'open and accessible as never before', identified a 'crucial problem' in the 'state of the Church in Christian countries'. In other words, the signs of spiritual recession within Europe itself were already clearly evident and led the writers of this report to warn that talk of the evangelization of the distant places on earth would prove futile 'unless there be a great expansion of vitality in the member churches of Christendom'. In a statement which now seems to contain an element of prophecy, the authors warned that the main concern of the conference should not be whether the peoples of the southern hemisphere would receive Christ, but whether Western Christians, 'in failing to communicate Him, *will themselves lose Him!*'[4]

The optimism which was so evident in Edinburgh in 1910 did not last long. Within the short space of four years the continent of Europe was to be engulfed in the bloodiest and most terrifying war experienced in human history, as the very nations which had been so proudly declared to be the heart of the 'Christianized world' at Edinburgh, fought each other with new and terrifying forms of mechanized weaponry. Every European nation was involved in this conflict except

---

4. Unpublished summary of Commission One of the World Missionary Conference, Edinburgh 1910, emphasis added. Summaries of each of the commission reports, together with important papers on 'Edinburgh, 1910' by a distinguished group of international scholars are available at <http://www.towards2010.org/papers.htm> (accessed 29 March 2012).

Spain, the Netherlands, Switzerland and the Scandinavian countries. The battle line between the combatants, the 'Western front', became 'a machine for massacre such as had probably never before been seen in the history of warfare'. Millions – *millions!* – of men faced each other from within trenches in which 'they lived like, and with, rats and lice'. The British, the French and the Germans all lost an entire generation in this conflict, with many towns in the north of England devastated by the deaths of so many young men under the age of thirty. Observers who tried to make sense of the chaos reached the conclusion that the world they had known, and of which they had been so proud and confident, was disintegrating before their eyes. As one historian of the period puts it, 'the great edifice of nineteenth-century civilization crumpled in the flames of war, as its pillars collapsed'.[5]

The impact of what came to be called the First World War on Western missions is seen most clearly in the reaction of one of the key players in the Edinburgh Conference, the Scottish layman, J. H. Oldham. Like most of his contemporaries, he was taken by surprise at the speed with which Europe descended into chaos and confessed that hardly anyone who had been present in the Edinburgh conference had anticipated the coming disaster. He struggled to understand the events through which he was living but recognized that they threatened to utterly destroy all he had been working for in mission over many years. Oldham insisted that the rising tide of nationalism and anti-Germanism in Britain should not be allowed to destroy 'the international fellowship and love which we began to learn at Edinburgh'. He wrote to Christians across the war-torn continent, including those in Germany,

5. Eric Hobsbawm, *Age of Extremes: The Short Twentieth Century,* *1914–1991* (London: Abacus, 1995), p. 22.

seeking to reaffirm and strengthen a unity in Christ transcending the widening chasm of racial divisions. Even more significant was Oldham's theological conclusion that modern Europe could not expect 'to escape the consequences of its sin'. He increasingly understood that the continent which the Edinburgh conference had so confidently declared to be 'evangelized' was, in fact, shaped by profound evils, and that 'the whole commercial system of the West' had resulted in deep social divisions and was one of the 'chief influences that . . . fostered national antagonisms'.[6]

As the war dragged on and the scale of the casualties increased to horrifying levels, Oldham's perceptions of mission began to change. When the full extent of Western moral bankruptcy became clear to him, the model of mission that underlay the Edinburgh conference, namely that Europe was a Christianized continent with a superior civilization which it was obligated to extend across the globe, lay exposed as a terrible mistake. Oldham was forced to the conclusion that, although Christendom continued to send thousands of missionaries to the southern continents, it 'had all but lost its credibility and moral authority for engaging in such an enterprise'.[7] By January 1915, Joe Oldham can be found writing the following remarkable passage:

> I cannot help thinking that the war is teaching us to draw a
> clear distinction between the Church of Christ and what we
> have been accustomed to speak of as Christian civilization.
> We have assumed that we had a 'Christian civilization' which
> was something we could proudly offer to the non-Christian

---

6. Keith Clements, *Faith on the Frontier. A Life of J. H. Oldham*
   (Edinburgh: T&T Clark, 1999), p. 125.

7. Ibid., p. 135.

world. *God is showing us how rotten that civilization is.* We shall need in future to be more humble, to be more ready to take up the cross, follow Christ and bear his reproach among men.[8]

J. H. Oldham

The end of Christendom . . . but not of Christ!

Joe Oldham's realization that European civilization would need to be clearly distinguished from the message of the gospel of Christ anticipated discussions concerning the gospel and culture which were to become key themes in missionary theology in the second half of the twentieth century. However, the legacy of the identification of Christianity with European, or Western, civilization continues to create serious misunderstanding and confusion and, especially on the volatile fault lines where the gospel encounters Islam, demands rigorous

---

8. Ibid., p. 140, emphasis added.

and critical theological reflection. Indeed, I wish to argue that there are reasons to believe that this issue is now more urgent than at any previous time.[9]

First, within the old Christian heartlands in Europe the gap between faith and culture has grown ever wider in the course of the twentieth century, with the result that any failure to distinguish Christ and the gospel from the profoundly materialistic system which now dominates this continent will have catastrophic results for the Christian mission. Since the First World War revealed the extent to which European Christianity had lost critical contact with its own culture, the crisis of faith in the West has continually deepened. Jane Collier and Rafael Esteban describe how Christendom used the political and economic expansion of Europe as the vehicle for its global mission with little evidence of condemnation of the colonial enterprise. They continue,

> But while the churches were using their energy happily growing in the territories opened to them by colonization, they failed to realize that in their own Western back yard an alternative culture was emerging that was to claim the adherence of church members, body and soul, by its promises of instant success and gratification, and the elimination of all evils afflicting humanity. Science and the invisible hand of the

9. Nearly thirty years ago, Jan H. Boer attempted precisely such a critical theological evaluation of missions and Western culture in his *Missions: Heralds of Capitalism or Christ?* (Ibadan: Daystar Press, 1984). I gratefully acknowledge my indebtedness to this book, but the need for a fresh, broader evaluation of the impact of Western culture on Christianity in both Africa and Europe itself is now urgent in the light of globalization.

market would gradually replace God and God's providence in the hearts of believers.[10]

By the end of the twentieth century, and after yet another bloodbath which devastated both East and West and left us with the seemingly insoluble legacy of the Holocaust, the decline of European Christianity reached a level at which whole swathes of institutional and denominational forms of the church were barely surviving. At the same time, mosques were becoming prominent features on the skylines of every major British city, while militant forms of unbelief and atheism gained ground in public discourses, whether through the educational system or the increasingly powerful mass media. However, notwithstanding the significance of these changes, the core ideology which now reigned largely un-challenged over this culture was what Oldham had called 'the commercial system of the West', or what we have heard Lesslie Newbigin describe as the ideology of the 'free market'. When the Communist regimes in Russia and Eastern Europe collapsed in 1989, bringing to an end the bi-polar world of East and West which had begun with the Russian revolution in 1917, the capitalist market system was left free to expand without challenge. Voices were now heard in prominent places in Europe and North America declaring the 'triumph of the West' and the 'end of history'. This was the prelude to the emergence of the phenomenon of *globalization*, the near-universal reach of a market system with its roots deep in the history of the Western world, a system which is accompanied by promises of human development and well-being, but

---

10. Jane Collier and Rafael Esteban, *From Complicity to Encounter: The Church and the Culture of Economism* (Harrisburg: Trinity Press International, 1998), p. 48.

which in reality condemns millions of poor people to life in ever-expanding urban slums.[11] For Christians in Europe and North America who continue to benefit economically from this system, the supreme challenge of the present age remains that suggested by Joe Oldham more than a century ago, namely, *to disentangle the gospel from the all-pervasive technical and economic culture in which we 'live and move and have our being', so that we might rediscover the meaning of the death of Jesus and walk in his way.*

Second, even as the influence of Christendom waned in Europe, to the point at which a new generation of young people in post-war Germany could say, 'We have forgotten that we have forgotten God', the message of the gospel was being received with joy by millions of people across the southern continents. Andrew Walls has pointed out that the dreams and visions of the Edinburgh Conference concerning the evangelization of the 'non-Christian world' were fulfilled, although 'not in the way, nor always by the means, nor even in the places that the delegates expected and planned'. But the twentieth century witnessed a huge reversal of the position in 1910, resulting in a situation in which today 'the majority of Christians now live in Africa, Asia, Latin America or the Pacific'.[12] The biggest surprise of all has been the growth of

---

11. See *The State of the World's Cities 2006/2007. The Millennium Development Goals and Urban Sustainability: 30 Years of Shaping the Habitat Agenda* (London: Earthscan, 2007). 'The year 2007 will also see the number of slum dwellers in the world cross the one billion mark – when one in every three city residents will live in inadequate housing with no or few basic services', p. viii.

12. Andrew Walls, unpublished paper 'The Great Commission 1910–2010', at 'Towards 2010 Conference' <http://www.towards2010.org/papers.htm> (accessed 2 April 2012). See also his 'From

Christianity across sub-Saharan Africa. Of the 1,215 delegates present at the Edinburgh conference, less than twenty came from the non-Western world and *none of these were from Africa.*[13] Yet in the course of the twentieth century the number of Christians in Africa grew, and went on growing, so that it is now estimated that something over 300 million people on this continent profess to be Christians. Many observers have recognized that sub-Saharan Africa has become one of the new Christian heartlands, quietly replacing Europe as the centre of spiritual and theological life and renewal within the worldwide Body of Christ.

Christendom to World Christianity', in *The Cross-Cultural Process in Christian History* (Edinburgh: T&T Clark, 2002), pp. 49–71. Philip Jenkins has discussed this paradigm shift in a series of volumes as follows: *The Next Christendom: The Coming of Global Christianity* (New York: Oxford University Press, 2002); *The New Faces of Christianity: Believing the Bible in the Global South* (New York: Oxford University Press, 2006); and *God's Continent: Christianity, Islam, and Europe's Religious Crisis* (New York: Oxford University Press, 2007). An African perspective on Christianity, the West and globalization is provided by Lamin Sanneh in *Encountering the West: Christianity and the Global Cultural Process: The African Dimension* (London: Marshall Pickering, 1993).

13. Brian Stanley has discovered a previously unknown 'additional African delegate' in the person of M. C. Hayford, the member of a distinguished Euro-African family from the Gold Coast. Stanley explains the absence of Africans as due to the fact that the inhabitants of this continent were still viewed as 'primitive' and at an early stage of evolutionary development, consequently Africa was seen as 'relatively unimportant for the future of the world church', *The World Missionary Conference*, pp. 97–99.

While I do not wish to deny or in any way diminish the significance of the shift in the centre of gravity in world Christianity which scholars like Walls have so well described, important questions need to be raised concerning the impact of modern, Western culture, especially in the era of globalization, on the burgeoning churches of the Global South. Looking back across the twentieth century, and before the term 'globalization' had entered our vocabulary, the historian Theodore von Laue described what he called 'the world revolution of Westernization'. A global rivalry for wealth and power had 'stimulated an unprecedented rise in material prosperity' and advanced 'human mobility', creating a 'global metropolis remarkably uniform in appearance and standards, glittering with the splendour of human ingenuity'. Yet von Laue warned that this global city was increasingly populated by people full of 'deadly fears and explosive anger' resulting from the 'depths of despair, frustration, and fury to which the world revolution of Westernization has reduced its victims'. Using biblical imagery, von Laue concluded that the worldwide confluence brought about by the modern market system 'has produced not a shiny global city but a global tower of Babel in which the superficial and ignorant comparison of everything with everything else is undermining all subtle distinctions between right and wrong, good and evil, worth and worthlessness'. Where, he asked, in this global Babylon do we find 'the transcendent moral absolutes that can restrain the rising penchant for violence?'[14]

With that penetrating and crucially important question we reach the end of this introductory survey, because it brings us

---

14. Theodore von Laue, *The World Revolution of Westernization. The Twentieth Century in Global Perspective* (New York: Oxford University Press, 1987), pp. 7–8.

from Edinburgh, 1910, to Jos, Nigeria, 2012. The 'deadly fears and explosive anger' mentioned by von Laue are tragic realities in this African city at the present time and they create precisely the context for mission in a *troubled* world which is our concern in these studies. In many ways Jos is a microcosm of the world described by von Laue and other commentators. As a post-colonial city it owes its very existence to the expansion of European power in the nineteenth and twentieth centuries, with the complex and ambivalent legacy which such an origin inevitably involves. But in addition, it sits on the fault line between African Christianity and Islam, so that the struggle for the allegiance of hearts and minds between the three worldviews which Newbigin suggested would shape the twenty-first century *is taking place within this city.* As a result, the form which the Christian mission takes here has a significance which extends far beyond the Nigerian Plateau, and indeed well beyond Nigeria.

At the conclusion of his massive study of the global impact of Western modernism, Theodore von Laue again resorted to biblical imagery, describing 'the Babylonian confusion' which 'encourages a shrinkage of moral sensibility through a relapse into a divisive and self-righteous fundamentalism, whether in religion or politics'. Lamenting the loss of any overarching and universal truth, he warned of the perils which lay ahead if 'impassioned fundamentalists of incompatible convictions' failed to communicate with each other and retreated behind the closed walls of their own absolute certainties. His closing question might be read as suggesting the agenda for these studies: 'How is it possible to establish common ground with strangers across the barriers of cultural incomprehension and ingrained political hostility? How can one get to the other side?[15]

---

15. Ibid., pp. 366–367.

While it might be assumed that the primary application of such questions concerns the Christian approach to Islam, I want to propose that in truth the most urgent dialogue is that which needs to take place with the advocates of modernization and Westernization, and that therefore our primary task is to *reflect on the degree to which the fundamentally secular assumptions of the ideology of market economics may have distorted our understanding of the message of the gospel and compromised our mission.* Might it be the case that as we engage in serious critical reflection on this frontier, we may reach conclusions which then open up previously unrecognized spaces for conversation with our Muslim neighbours, revealing a surprising new pathway 'to the other side' which we have never noticed before?

2

Critical issues concerning
the gospel and culture

The relationship between the gospel and culture has been a
central theme of missionary theology during the second half
of the twentieth century. In part this was the result of the
experiences of Western missionaries at the intersections of
cultures in many different parts of the world, experiences
which were sometimes painful and embarrassing. There is a
large fund of stories relating misunderstandings arising either
from a failure to read cultural symbols correctly, or because
of linguistic mistakes, often the result of mistranslations
capable of arousing the fury of listeners or reducing them to
helpless laughter. Chinua Achebe provides a classic example
of the latter in his great novel *Things Fall Apart*, describing
how an interpreter with limited knowledge of the local Igbo
dialect rendered the English term 'myself' by a local word
that meant 'my buttocks', creating an outbreak of hilarity
among the audience and reducing the missionary's credibility
to zero! More seriously, cross-cultural communication has
often been blocked by actions which carried profoundly
significant meanings within the receptor culture of which the

missionary was completely unaware. Take the example of a missionary couple who endeavoured to work in a remote village in North India. The local people were astonished to observe that the foreigners had brought a cat with them and that they kept this animal within their house. In this culture cats carried a very particular meaning since they were only ever kept by witches, and it was believed that they were used to steal people's souls while they slept. On the first occasion that the missionary addressed the men of the village, completely unaware of the anxious discussions which his cat had provoked, he announced, 'I have come to win your souls for Christ'! The astonishment on the faces of the village elders led the missionary to believe he had communicated well, but the elders were wondering *who was this Christ, and what did he want with their souls!*[1]

Experiences like these led to the recognition of the difficulties of cross-cultural communication and the crucial importance of gaining as accurate an understanding of receptor cultures as possible. The discipline signified by the term 'missiology' incorporated insights from social anthropology, communications science and linguistics in the search for the knowledge and skills which might minimize misunderstanding at the frontiers of culture. However, the deeper the engagement with receptor cultures became, the more complex and challenging the entire process appeared to be, since the discovery of non-Western, traditional ways of understanding reality often led to the exposure of previously unrecognized blind spots in the missionaries' own reading of the Bible. In other words, the process of

---

1. The story is taken from Robert Schreiter, *The New Catholicism: Theology Between the Global and the Local* (New York: Orbis Books, 2004), p. 33.

contextualization was often discovered to be profoundly disturbing in that, instead of being a one-way process in which the 'pure' gospel was implanted in alien cultural soils, it triggered entirely unanticipated critical questions concerning the relationship between the message of Christ and the missionary's own culture. Culture thus became challenging at both ends of the process of communication as mission shone fresh light on both receptor and sending cultural contexts. This experience, which so clearly reflects the struggle of the apostle Peter to come to terms with the *missio Dei* in his encounter with the Gentile world in the person of the god-fearing Cornelius, transcends denominational traditions, as the reaction of Roman Catholic missionaries in the north of Ghana so strikingly reveals. Their experience among the Dagomba people revealed that there were traditional African ways of being human 'that overflowed with life-loving and a life-giving energy', and showed that God was already present, unexpectedly, 'in the middle of Africa'. These Catholic missionaries concluded that both existing European models of mission and the Roman Catholic idea of 'a perfect "teaching" church' had to be given up!

> What we discover in the missionary encounter is first of all that the church is far from perfect and – much more important – that it has everything to learn from and about the peoples whom it intends to evangelize. The missionary experience shows that God is more mysterious than we thought and does not play by our rules.[2]

---

2. Jane Collier and Rafael Esteban, *From Complicity to Encounter, The Church and the Culture of Economism* (Harrisburg: Trinity Press International, 1998), p. 86.

Civilization, mission and syncretism

While the lessons learned by Western missionaries at the frontiers with other cultures across the southern hemisphere were obviously important, it is the challenge posed to the gospel by the culture from which the missionaries themselves came, namely the technical, scientific worldview stemming from the European Enlightenment, which is our primary concern. If people like Joe Oldham were correct in their judgment that the civilization stemming from this worldview was *rotten,* what does this mean with regard to the form in which the gospel was brought to Africa by missionaries educated and socialized in nineteenth- and twentieth-century Europe? And did the churches which resulted from such missionary activity themselves become infected by whatever aspects of the sending culture are now recognized as being erroneous, or even potentially dangerous to social harmony and human well-being? Finally, what might this mean for relationships with Muslims? When they appear to be repudiating the message of Christ, is it in fact the gospel they are reacting against, or rather is it those elements of a form of Christianity which is the carrier of aspects of Western modernity and secularism, elements which are alien to Christ and should never have been presented as part of the gospel in the first place? In a divided and troubled nation such as Nigeria we are compelled to ask whether Muslim antipathy toward the churches and their expansion is, at least in part, the result of a profound fear that Christianity is the Trojan horse for the expansion of Western cultural and economic dominance and the undermining of the ethical and religious values which are integral to the Islamic vision of society.[3]

---

3. There is a large body of literature which explores the many and complex factors involved in the running crisis in the Middle Belt

I wish to explore these critical questions in relation to two specific aspects of modern, Western culture which enable us to sharpen the focus of this discussion. The first concerns the divorce between economics and ethics which is the direct outcome of the eighteenth-century European Enlightenment. At the dawn of the industrial revolution in Britain economics came to be understood as a rational, scientific discipline by means of which the laws believed to govern wealth creation might be discovered. The discovery of such laws would, it was thought, reveal the path to previously unknown national and individual prosperity. Since modern economics was believed to deal with scientific knowledge, it gained enormous credibility and prestige in a society in which science was recognized as the supreme source of true facts, in distinction to mere beliefs or superstitions. At the same time, the advance of economics was accompanied by the *retreat of theology*. God's place within the emerging worldview was strictly limited and over the course of the nineteenth- and twentieth-centuries would disappear altogether.

---

of Nigeria, especially on the Jos Plateau. See Sunday Bobai Agang, *The Impact of Ethnic, Political and Religious Violence on Northern Nigeria, and a Theological Reflection on its Healing* (Carlisle: Langham Monographs, 2011); Jan H. Boer, *Nigeria's Decades of Blood 1980–2002* (Ontario: Essence Publishing, 2003); Ulrika Andersson Trovalla, *Medicine for Uncertain Futures: A Nigerian City in the Wake of a Crisis* (Uppsala: Uppsala Universitet, 2011); and Umar Habila Dadem Danfulani, 'The Jos Peace Conference and the Indigene/Settler Question in Nigerian Politics', <http://www.ascleiden.nl/Pdf/paper-Danfulani.pdf> (accessed 26 July 2012). On ethnic, religious and political tensions within Nigeria more generally, see Toyin Falola, *Violence in Nigeria: The Crisis of Religious Politics and Secular Ideologies* (Rochester NY: University of Rochester Press, 1998).

In the city of Glasgow, Scotland, in 1709, at the beginning of a massive expansion of trade and prosperity, we discover Christians lamenting the feverish pursuit of wealth and the diminishing influence of Christian ethics among those engaged in commercial activity. Yet, while a theologian like Robert Woodrow warned his contemporaries that allowing trade to subvert religion would bring tragedy and judgment upon the city, few took much notice of such words because biblical principles were being eclipsed by the view that 'business affairs should be left to be settled by business men, unhampered by the intrusions of an antiquated morality or by misconceived arguments of public policy'.[4] In time this divorce between ethics and commercial and economic life would result in the end of Christendom and its replacement by what has been called *a culture of economism*. That is to say, the Western world came to be dominated by an ideology in which economic causes replaced religion as 'the main source of cultural meanings and values' and provided the 'ordinary-language terms and expressions' with which modern people give meaning to daily life.[5]

---

4. These words are from R. H. Tawney, *Religion and the Rise of Capitalism* (London: John Murray, 1936), pp. 238–239. For more on the erosion of ethics in the commercial life of the city of Glasgow see my *Seeking a City With Foundations: Theology for an Urban World* (Nottingham: IVP, 2012), especially pp. 105–115.

5. Collier and Esteban, *From Complicity to Encounter*, pp. 16–17. On the history of the developments briefly outlined here, see Bob Goudzwaard, *Capitalism and Progress: A Diagnosis of Western Society* (Carlisle: Paternoster Press, 1979); Donald Hay and Alan Kreider (eds.), *Christianity and the Culture of Economics* (Cardiff: University of Wales Press, 2001). John Atherton's *Christianity and the Market. Christian Social Thought for Our Times* (London: SPCK,

The crucial issue for us concerns the role played by Christian theology in this momentous historical development. The retreat of theology in the face of the unstoppable advance of the ideology of market economics was not simply a matter of new, modern ideas replacing an outdated and antiquated religious worldview (as the defenders of modern culture would like to believe), but rather, it involved the co-option by the Enlightenment thinkers of the language and attributes which had previously been ascribed to God himself. As Douglas Meeks has observed, while modern economics refused to speak of God, the language with which it described the operation of the market suggested 'another level of reality', so that market forces came to determine human social and political life in much the same manner that divine providence was once believed to operate. As Meeks puts it,

> Attributes that denote domination within the market are residues of Western conceptions of divinity that still function as the uncontested assumptions of our society. These concepts at one time justified the unlimitedness of political rulership . . . Now, applied to the nature of the human being, they justify the unlimitedness of the power which is formed through the process of accumulation in market society.[6]

1992) provides a good description of differing Christian responses to market economics, including the conservative defence of the free market on the grounds that it is both efficient and results in greater human freedom. This is the argument of Brian Griffiths, an evangelical Christian who was economic policy advisor to Margaret Thatcher in Downing Street.

6. M. Douglas Meeks, *God the Economist: The Doctrine of God and Political Economy* (Minneapolis: Fortress Press, 1989), p. 65. I owe much to the rich insights of this important, sadly neglected, book.

In other words, the language once used of God in classical theology – transcendence, omnipotence, immutability – was transferred to human actors, so that even if the essence of the 'imperial God' was dead in Western culture, his attributes remained alive in the modern market concept of the human being. 'Once the metaphysical attributes are no longer applied to an eternal essence, they are reappropriated by the human being.' In the modern world, therefore, the spheres of politics and economics operate at the formal level without reference to God, but the now sovereign power of the market 'depends upon coercive conceptions once applied to God but now given as the presuppositions of the market human being'.[7] European philosophers recognized, sometimes with celebration, at other times with profound foreboding, that in the absence of God, human beings would need to take full responsibility for the governance of the world. At a much more mundane level, the transfer of power from heaven to earth is reflected in the title given today to those who operate the global economic systems from within the skyscrapers which dominate world cities; they are called, with little or no irony, the 'Masters of the Universe'.[8]

The question might be asked as to how the development we

---

7. Ibid.

8. The global economic crash in the early twenty-first century has alerted some secular commentators to these realities. Thus, Larry Elliott and Dan Atkinson wrote *The Gods That Failed: How Blind Faith in Markets Has Cost Us Our Future* (London: The Bodley Head, 2008). They describe how democratic governments have 'willingly ceded control of the world economy to a new elite of freebooting super-rich free market operatives' whom they describe as the 'New Olympians' – a title chosen because of 'their remoteness from everyday life, their lack of accountability and . . . the faith to which they subscribe', p. 4.

have outlined here can be reconciled to the fact that the same century which witnessed this massive cultural shift in Europe, and especially within the United Kingdom, has also been described as the 'evangelical century' and as the 'great century' of Christians missions?[9] The answer is that while the nineteenth century certainly witnessed significant church growth within industrializing and urbanizing societies, a growth which provided the base for an expanding overseas missionary work, the broader context was marked by a cultural split in which the critically important spheres of education, economics and politics were increasingly shaped by people whose worldview was uncompromisingly modernist. Meantime, many evangelical Christians acquiesced in this situation, accepting a dualistic theology which involved a retreat from the public square into the private world of the family and the individual. Indeed, it was precisely this apolitical form of Western Christianity, preoccupied with the eternal salvation of individual souls, which Lesslie Newbigin was to describe in 1983 as 'an advanced case of syncretism'.[10]

---

9. The first phrase comes from David Bebbington, *Evangelicalism in Modern Britain, A History From the 1730s to the 1980s* (London: Unwin Hyman, 1989), while the second forms part of the title of Kenneth Scott Latourette's *A History of the Expansion of Christianity, Volume IV – The Great Century in Europe and North America* (Grand Rapids: Zondervan, 1970).

10. Lesslie Newbigin, *The Other Side of 1984: Questions for the Churches* (Geneva: World Council of Churches, 1983), p. 24. Newbigin wrote, 'The typical form of living Christian faith in its Protestant forms from the eighteenth century onwards was pietism, a religion of the soul, of the inner life, of personal morals and the home . . . Christian faith became – for most people – a private and domestic matter strictly separated from the public worlds of politics and economics', p. 22.

If this outline of the relationship between European Christianity and the economistic culture which became increasingly dominant in twentieth-century Europe is accepted, and if it is reasonable to assume that a missionary movement emerging from such a context communicated the gospel to Africa in a form which reflected this situation, then it is not surprising that Muslims, who make no such divorce between faith and economic and political life, should express fears that the huge growth of the churches across this continent will have social, political and economic consequences which they find disturbing. To state the central issue as clearly as possible: *does Christianity bring social justice and righteousness where it wins converts, or does its concentration on personal salvation and the needs of individual souls, render it powerless to resist the immense forces unleashed by a global market economy?* Those forces are, I suggest, gathering strength in Africa at the present time, so that the questions raised here are of fundamental significance for the future of Christianity on this continent. According to the International Monetary Fund (IMF), the economies of sub-Saharan Africa were likely to grow in 2012 by 5.75%, with those regions which are rich in natural resources experiencing much greater rates of economic growth. The question is whether this increased wealth, accompanied by the accelerating pace of urbanization throughout the continent, will result in greater justice for the poor, or in a widening gap between a powerful and privileged urban elite and the millions of people confined to ever-expanding slums? And what role will African Christianity play in this scenario? Will it prove to be the Trojan horse for Western secularization,[11] or can it discover a more biblical

---

11. In a detailed examination of the history of Muslim-Christian tensions in Nigeria, Toyin Falola comments: 'Christianity created a new elite more attuned to the increasing spread of Western

theology than that inherited from European Christendom, and so become a socially transformative force for modern Africa? We will return to this question later, but suffice to say at this point that such a discovery would demand the recognition that the God revealed in the Bible is fundamentally concerned with political and socio-economic issues since they involve the out-working of the righteousness and justice which are key aspects of his own character. In the words of Douglas Meeks,

> God's economy is fundamentally about God's struggle with death, the power of the *nihil*. Will the cosmic household live or will it fall victim to God's enemy, death, which seeks in every moment to disrupt the distribution of righteousness in the household and thus to close out life? This is the pervasive question of the biblical traditions.[12]

---

civilization . . . The dominance of the Christian elite in the state bureaucracy . . . lent substantial support to the introduction of Western secular ideologies', *Violence in Nigeria*, p. 38. The increasingly powerful presence of secularizing forms of modernity in Africa's cities is reflected in newspaper reports of the 'Arise Africa' fashion week in Lagos. The success of this quintessentially modern event, in which catwalking African models displayed clothes described as 'strong, sexy and confident' for the benefit of the rich and wealthy, is said to have been such a success that Lagos may become 'a major fixture in the global fashion calendar', Monica Mark, 'Why Not Lagos? Fashion week triumph sees Africa's star rising', *The Guardian*, 13 March, 2012. Elsewhere the same newspaper reports on the yawning gap emerging between the super-rich of Lagos and Abuja and the mass of the nation's population: 'Full speed ahead for Africa's super-rich', *The Guardian*, 24 March, 2012.

12. Meeks, *God the Economist*, p. 77.

The source of knowledge

If the divorce between economics and ethics is one crucial aspect of the Western tradition which gives rise to Muslim concerns regarding Christianization, a second concerns the nature of human knowledge itself, a matter with serious implications in the realm of education. Lamin Sanneh, himself a Christian convert from Islam, describes how Muslim societies understand all human knowledge as embedded within a religious concept of reality. He quotes the famous Muslim scholar, al-Ghazali as saying: 'I sought knowledge without God, but God forbade it that knowledge should be without Him.' By contrast, Sanneh describes the Western approach to knowledge, which he traces back to the great Puritan, John Milton, as leading to 'an overweening confidence in the limitless human capacity to know'. On that basis education becomes 'the unfettered search for truth and the rolling back of the frontiers of ignorance'.[13] As we have already seen, during the eighteenth and nineteenth centuries in Europe confidence in the power of human reason increased with the emergence of modern science, so that a secular and

---

13. Lamin Sanneh, *The Crown and the Turban. Muslims and West African Pluralism* (Boulder, Colorado: Westview Press, 1997), pp. 117–118. See also this author's *Piety and Power: Muslims and Christians in West Africa* (New York: Orbis Books, 1996). There is some overlap of material in these two volumes. Sanneh's *Encountering the West: Christianity and the Global Cultural Process – The African Dimension* (London: Marshall Pickering, 1993) is also directly relevant to this discussion as is his brilliant article, 'Christianity, Politics and Citizenship with Reference to Africa: A Comparative Enquiry', *Journal of African Christian Thought* 14/1, June 2011, pp. 3–19.

Lamin Sanneh

materialist approach to knowledge came to be regarded as superior to traditional ways of learning. Indeed, the confidence of Western intellectuals that their ways of knowing provided a unique and privileged access to truth and reality meant that education became almost a secular gospel to be shared across a still-benighted world through the agency of colonial power and empire. As Sanneh observes, in the modern West free intellectual enquiry came to be understood as 'the greatest safeguard against bigotry, intolerance, repression, and conformity' and the spread of such ideas took the form of a 'high and holy calling'. When the Western colonial powers encountered non-Western cultures they attempted to refashion them in their own 'archetypal image', but 'nowhere has this encounter been more riddled with misunderstanding, more fraught with tension than in the field of Muslim education'. From the Muslim side it appeared that the West 'was determined to cut asunder the venerable cord of religion and learning that Allah had knit'.[14]

The resistance of Islam to the secularized pattern of education which entered Africa during the colonial period further helps to explain Muslim anxieties regarding Christian missionary activity because Western missionary organizations became the primary providers of secular education. Indeed, the provision of education on a Western model of knowledge 'became the most noticeable aspect of missions in Africa'.[15] Even strongly conservative, evangelical groups which had initially claimed that their exclusive calling was evangelistic and 'spiritual', ended up under colonial conditions building schools and colleges to deliver educational programmes that met the colonial government's standards and objectives and delivered externally devised curricula. Harry Boer observed that the schools founded by Western missions often ended up serving very different purposes from what had been originally intended, and that many who attended them 'desired and

14. *The Crown and the Turban*, p. 118. In ch. 6 of this book, with the title 'A Childhood Muslim Education', Sanneh movingly describes his own experience of being nurtured in a deeply Muslim culture and the shock of his encounter with Western, secular education. He concludes: you 'cannot throw children from the old system into the new without producing an identity crisis. That is why generations of children in traditional society arrived in the new world of Western secularism with a sense of dissonance and alienation', p. 146.

15. Andrew Walls, *The Cross-Cultural Process in Christian History* (Edinburgh: T&T Clark, 2002), pp. 97–98. The chapter from which this quotation is taken is entitled 'Africa in Christian History' and is a very important survey of this subject.

found only intellectual and material advancement'.[16] In other words, *missionary schools were the unwitting agents of secularization!* By contrast, Muslim communities were 'unwilling to make Muslim education tools of Western-inspired social and economic development' since, as Sanneh puts it, they 'set far more store by education than merely viewing it as a passport to a career'.[17]

The characteristic Western divorce between the realms of the sacred and the secular, largely accepted without demur by European Christians and by the missionary societies associated with them, would seem to have been a major source of misunderstandings, tension and conflict in the relationships between African Christians and Muslims in Nigeria. The growth in the Christian population, from a mere 6% in 1931, to around 45% by the beginning of this century, heightened Muslim fears that the evangelistic success of the churches represented the advance guard of an alien economic and political culture. These anxieties could only be increased by the fact that much of this expansion was achieved by Christian

16. Harry Boer, *Pentecost and Missions* (Grand Rapids: Eerdmans, 1961), p. 229.

17. Sanneh, *The Crown and the Turban*, p. 3. In a study of 'Middle Belt Christianity' in Nigeria, Niels Kastfelt comments that education became the 'most important field of co-operation' between the British colonial power and Christian missions. 'For economic reasons the British were unable to train as many Nigerians as were needed to staff the lower levels of the colonial bureaucracy, and [they] therefore turned to the mission schools and came to rely strongly on the missionary educational system, which the administrators saw as an important agent of social and economic innovation', Niels Kastfelt, *Religion and Politics in Nigeria: A Study in Middle Belt Christianity* (London: British Academic Press, 1994), p. 22.

groups displaying overt hostility toward Islam and using language which both reawakened painful historical memories of the crusades and frequently characterized Islam as demonic. Some at least of this Christianity has strong links with fundamentalist groups in the United States and, while the 'dynamics of interreligious tension in Nigeria are enormously complex', it is reasonable to conclude that one contributory factor 'is the kind of Christianity' which has engaged in aggressive, theologically shallow, evangelism in the north of the country.[18]

We are left with a series of questions regarding mission in our troubled world. Lesslie Newbigin's claim that the three worldviews which will compete for the allegiance of the human family in the twenty-first century would be the gospel, Islam, and the ideology of the free market, compels us to enquire what Christian mission looks like at the intersection with those two frontiers? With regard to Islam, I suggest we must move beyond negative stereotypes of this tradition if we are to be able to appreciate the real nature and extent of the challenge which it represents to a Christianity which has lost the vision of social transformation within the biblical narratives. Andrew Walls' sobering words should be pondered:

> Nor should we underestimate the appeal of the preaching of Islam, the sense of Islamic kinship, and the ideal of the Islamic

---

18. Steve Brower, Paul Gifford and Susan Rose, *Exporting the American Gospel: Global Christian Fundamentalism* (London: Routledge, 1996). I disagree strongly with some of the conclusions of these authors in that they attribute far too much influence to American forms of Christianity in modern Africa. A more balanced survey is found in Paul Freston, *Evangelicals and Politics in Asia, Africa and Latin America* (Cambridge: Cambridge University Press, 2001).

state where justice is performed according to the way of God. For many poor, downtrodden people, helpless against outside forces, surrounded by corruption, and the conspicuous consumption of the wealthy, the ugly face of the Western world in the midst, the call to radical obedience to Allah brings the stirring hope of a better day that Marxism once evoked.[19]

Do we not hear in this statement a call, not to retreat and timidity, but to repentance at our failure to honour and serve the God revealed to us in Christ, and to renewed faithfulness to the traditions of biblical Israel and the crucified Messiah, in whom God's kingdom of justice, mercy and *shalom* has broken into our history with the promise of the healing and blessing of all the nations on earth? This call comes to all of us, but allow me to suggest that Christianity in Africa may be the bearer of a particular missionary vocation at this point in the history of the world. The theology of church and state which we have inherited from the past was developed during the long era of Christendom in Europe and is now wholly inadequate to meet the challenges posed by both political Islam and the global force of market capitalism. Andrew Walls suggests that African Christian theologians may bear responsibility today for the construction 'of new theologies of the political and economic realm that we [all] need'. It is precisely from the African context, and perhaps even more particularly from Jos, that fresh Christian thinking may be forged in the heat of the tensions arising at the frontier with Islam, responding creatively to the urgent questions which that dialogue raises for us, while also facing the terrible realities of human suffering and oppression across this great continent. As Walls suggests, from this crucible may emerge 'a theology

19. Walls, *The Cross-Cultural Process*, p. 112.

for the World Bank – indeed, perhaps a theology of banking – that the whole world needs'.[20] In that process we are likely to find that previously undiscovered spaces for conversation with Muslims will open up, enabling us both to learn from them how 'religion and politics, church and state, the private and the public have much to do with each other',[21] while at the same time those 'paths to the other side' will enable us to bear humble and credible testimony to the Lamb of God, who alone is worthy to take and open the scroll which represents the unfolding history of our world, and 'to receive power and wealth and wisdom and strength and honour and glory and praise!' (Rev. 5:12).

---

20. Ibid., p. 113. In the 1984 study referenced earlier, Jan Boer concluded that African Christianity had largely overlooked the resources provided by traditional religion, Islam and – most of all – the Bible for the development of a holistic theology. The dualistic theology which confined religion to the private sphere 'caused missions to go astray in their support of capitalism and colonialism', *Missions: Heralds of Capitalism or Christ?*, p. 144.
21. Sanneh, *Piety and Power*, p. 48.

3

Mission, violence and suffering

On 2 March, 2011, the Pakistani government minister for minorities, Shahbaz Bhatti, was shot dead outside his mother's home in Islamabad. He was forty-two years old and had been a courageous opponent of Pakistan's blasphemy laws and the injustice and intolerance which they encouraged. Bhatti was a Roman Catholic who had experienced a spiritual awakening as a young man which led him to dedicate his life to the service of other people, especially the poor and oppressed, in imitation of Jesus Christ. He founded a political party called the Christian Liberation Front in 1985 while studying for a postgraduate degree in political science. He was a man who, in a context of violence and great danger, had a vision; he believed that Pakistan could become a beacon of tolerance and harmony and to this end, in his own words, he wanted 'to make this world beautiful by delivering a message of peace, togetherness, unity and tolerance'. After his death a taped message was discovered which he had recorded in the knowledge that his life was in danger. This is what it said:

The forces of violence, militant banned organizations, the Taliban and pro al-Qaida, they want to impose their radical philosophy in Pakistan and whoever stands against their radical philosophy, they threaten them.

When I'm leading this campaign against *sharia* law, for the abolishment of the blasphemy law and speaking for the oppressed and marginalized persecuted Christian and other minorities, these Taliban threaten me, but I want to share that I believe in Jesus Christ, who has given his own life for us.

I know what is the meaning of the cross and I'm following the cross and I'm ready to die for a cause.

I'm living for my community and the suffering people and I will die to defend their rights so these threats and these warnings cannot change my opinion and principles. I will prefer to die following my principle and for the justice of my community rather than compromise on these threats.[1]

'*I know what is the meaning of the cross!*' That statement, made by one of the bravest of Christian martyrs in modern times, has haunted me ever since I first read it and I want to suggest that it serves to highlight what is perhaps the central issue with regard to Christian mission in our troubled world today.

The death of Christ lies at the heart of the Christian faith and constitutes the very core of its missionary proclamation. Paul could sum up his gospel in the statement, 'we preach Christ crucified' (1 Cor. 1:23), before underlining the absolute centrality of the cross by telling the Corinthians, 'I resolved to know nothing while I was with you except Jesus Christ and

---

1. An obituary notice for Shahbaz Bhatti was published in *The Guardian*, 11 March 2011.

him crucified' (2:2). And yet the same apostle is clearly aware of the possibility that the *meaning* of the doctrine of the cross may be distorted in a manner which perverts and undermines the unique message of the gospel. Thus, he warns of the danger – present from the very beginning – that 'words of *human* wisdom' can domesticate the message of the cross and leave it 'emptied of its power' (1 Cor. 1:17). The history of Christian mission across two thousand years provides us with tragic examples of just such perversions, and the temptation to use the language of the cross without knowing its *power* remains very real in the divided and broken world of the twenty-first century.

Mission and the cross

I grew up singing hymns written by some of the great mystical theologians from the Middle Ages in Europe, most notably those of Bernard of Clairvaux (1091-1153). Here is an example:

Jesus, the very thought of Thee
With sweetness fills my breast;
But sweeter far Thy face to see,
And in Thy presence rest.

O hope of every contrite heart,
O joy of all the meek,
To those who ask, how kind Thou art!
How good to those who seek!

Jesus our only joy be Thou,
As Thou our prize shalt be;
In Thee be all our glory now,

And through eternity.

This is language which expresses a deep, spiritual devotion to Jesus and reflects the writer's awareness of the nature of Christianity as a way of life involving contrition, humility and meekness. Much later in my life I was deeply shocked to discover that the man who penned these beautiful words of heartfelt love for Jesus, was also a leading preacher of the crusading armies which marched across Europe to engage Muslims in fierce fighting for the ownership and control of the Holy Land and Jerusalem! Bernard of Clairvaux, hymn writer and a preacher who devoted more than eighty sermons to the theme of love in the Song of Songs, was also an advocate of holy wars against Muslims and promised the Christian crusaders who fought in these battles the remission of their sins. Christian soldiers were offered what amounted to a deal; in exchange for their military actions, they would receive both temporal and eternal blessings. 'This "good deal", to which repeated reference is made not just in crusading songs but also in the works of such distinguished preachers and theologians as Bernard of Clairvaux, was just part of the package of benefits which knightly participants hoped to acquire in joining the crusade.'[2]

How could this be? The answer to this question is deeply disturbing since it involves an example of precisely the perversion of the meaning of the cross of Christ with which, as we have seen, Paul was so concerned. The English word 'crusader' is a translation of the Latin term, *crucesignatus,*

---

2. Jeremy Johns, 'Christianity and Islam', in John MacManners (ed.), *The Oxford Illustrated History of Christianity* (Oxford: Oxford University Press, 1992), p. 172.

Shahbaz Bhatti

which means literally 'signed with the cross'. As is well known, the crusaders were indeed marked with the symbol of the cross; they wore it on their armour and it was engraved on their weapons, so that their battles were understood to be an extension of the conflict in which Christ had engaged and which brought him to the death of Calvary. Another preacher of the Crusades, Jacques de Vitry, said that just as Christ had been honoured after taking up his cross, so those who 'wear the same garments that their king wore and are signed with the same mark' will be greatly honoured. They, their wives and children, and even their dead parents, will be 'absolved from punishment of their sins in this world [and in eternity will be] safe from the tortures of hell, in the glory and honour of being crowned in eternal beatitude'.[3]

Here is a strange historical irony: in the twenty-first century it is Muslim Islamists who have shocked people across the Western world by their very public commitment to acts of

3. Quoted from Ida Glaser, *Crusade Sermons, Francis of Assisi and Martin Luther: What Does it Mean to 'Take Up The Cross' in the Context of Islam?*, Crowther Centre Monograph 14 (Oxford: Church Mission Society, 2008), pp. 8–9.

terror and violence and the belief that martyrdom in a sacred cause will be rewarded with the blessings of Paradise, and yet we discover precisely such beliefs prompting Christians to violence nine hundred years earlier, convinced that they had a contract with God which assured them of the blessings and rewards of heaven. This is far from being the only example of the ways in which the negative features of a contemporary non-Christian religion can be shown to have been present at an earlier stage in the history of the Christian tradition.

However, there were other Christian voices during the period of the crusades which called for a radically different approach to the Muslim world. The most famous, of course, was Francis of Assisi, who in 1219 travelled with the crusading army into Egypt, not in order to sanctify violence, but with the intention of showing an alternative way of relating to Muslims. Francis went with one companion into the camp of Sultan al-Kamil in order, as one study has put it, to 'wage peace on Islam'. The dialogue which took place between the Sultan and the unarmed Francis was cordial and resulted in Franciscans being welcomed in this Muslim kingdom, on the condition that they did not cause discord by speaking against Muhammed or the Qu'ran. When in the light of this experience, Francis later drew up the Rule for his order, it contained his mature thinking on mission to Islam. Permission to engage in such witness was to be given only to those Franciscans whom superiors could affirm as 'suitable to be sent'. In other words, the Franciscan Rule clearly recognized the sensitivities at this missionary frontier and the need to *exclude* certain people whose approach to mission and to Muslims was contrary to the way of Jesus Christ. Friars who crossed the cultural frontier with Islam were to 'conduct themselves spiritually', which meant not provoking arguments or strife, and being subject 'to every human creature for God's sake'.

This last phrase is based on 1 Peter 2:13, which is an apostolic instruction with clear political implications, requiring submission to ruling powers. In the era of the crusades this is a remarkable requirement since it clearly indicates that Christians are to respect and obey Islamic laws when they reside in Muslim territory! The most challenging aspect of the approach of Francis of Assisi to Islam, made all the more remarkable given the spirit of his age, concerns his imitation of Christ in the actual practice of the *love of ones' enemies*. Ida Glaser identifies the questions which this poses to Christians at the missionary frontier with Islam:

> The challenge to Christians today is whether we too will see our discipleship in terms of helping to establish and defend a political entity, or whether we will walk in the way of compassion and mercy of the Jesus we meet in the New Testament. . . . [I]t is only as we face this Gospel challenge that we can begin to take Christ-honouring roles in determining the policies of both Church and state in relationship to the range of challenges presented by Islam.[4]

The Franciscan requirement of respect for, and obedience to, Muslim authority when resident in territory governed by Islamic law brings us to another example of Christian missionary practice in which this same principle was followed. We move forward some 600 years to 1807 and to Yorubaland, in what is now Nigeria. A boy born in this year was named Ajayi and, according to a story told later, was devoted at birth to the service of Olurun, the high god of the Yoruba. When the boy was thirteen years old his community was raided by Fulani Muslims and he was led away captive, eventually being

4. Ibid., p. 32

sold to Portuguese slave traders at the coast. We may imagine the distress of this young man, the image of the burning houses of his home town, and the slaughter of the old people judged unfit to be traded as slaves, seared into his memory, and the fear of the unknown future as the Portuguese ship on which he now found himself set sail for the Atlantic Ocean. However, in April 1822 the slave ship was intercepted by a British naval squadron and Ajayi was taken, along with thousands of other homeless, disoriented Africans who had been released from slavery, to the newly founded colony of Sierra Leone. We know little of his early experience in this new community which was shaped by missionary Christianity and Western models of education, but after three years he was baptized by an Anglican missionary and given the name Samuel Crowther. He became one of the first students at Fourah Bay College in Freetown, an institution which offered the first university degrees to students in tropical Africa and had a huge influence in subsequent years.

The story of Samuel Ajayi Crowther's life and ministry is truly extraordinary and we cannot retell it here. He was ordained into the Anglican ministry in 1843, pioneered a mission in his native Yorubaland at Abeokuta, and played a key role in the translation of the Bible into Yoruba, a translation which 'set new standards for later African translations'.[5] Amazingly, during his missionary work among the Yoruba, Crowther was reunited with his mother and sister, from whom he had been so brutally parted thirty years earlier, and they were among the first people to be baptized in Abeokuta. In 1864 Crowther became the first African to be ordained as

---

5. Andrew Walls, 'Crowther, Samuel Adjai (or Ajayi)', in Gerald Anderson (ed.), *Biographical Dictionary of Christian Missions* (New York: MacMillan Reference USA, 1998), pp. 160–161.

Samuel Ajayi Crowther

an Anglican bishop, but what is of most interest to us is his encounter with Muslims, especially during a famous mission on the Niger which brought him into contact with the Emir of Ilorin in 1872.

Previous attempts to evangelize Muslims in Sierra Leone had convinced Crowther that merely to present doctrinal claims and counter claims about contentious issues invariably ended in shouting matches and achieved little or nothing of any value. Consequently, he undertook deep and sustained study of the Qur'an and looked for points of contact between it and the Bible. His discussions with Muslim hosts in the court at Ilorin are a model of dialogical mission, and they concluded with the Muslim ruler requesting Crowther to pray for the Emir and his people. Here surely is an amazing event; the man whose early life had been so brutally disrupted by Muslim raiders, now standing as the representative of Christ before an Islamic court and asked to pray for them! Crowther, as a good Anglican, turned to his Prayer Book and found a 'Prayer for the Queen's Majesty'. He explained however that when the prayer was used in territory beyond the sovereignty of Queen Victoria, her name was to be replaced 'by the name of the sovereign in whose dominions we are living'. In other words, it could be used as a prayer for the Emir and his court, and the Muslim ruler was given the assurance that Christians within his territory would pray for him in these terms! Here is an extract from that prayer:

> O Lord, our heavenly Father, high and mighty, King of kings, Lord of lords, the only ruler of princes, who dost from Thy throne behold all the dwellers on earth, . . . we beseech Thee with Thy favour to behold our most gracious Sovereign Lady, Queen Victoria [here read: the Emir of Ilorin]; and so replenish her [him] with the grace of Thy Holy Spirit, that she [he] may incline always to Thy will, and walk in Thy way . . .[6]

This prayer met with the approval of the Emir. There is, of course, a tragic end to the story of Samuel Ajayi Crowther because, at the end of his life, a new generation of British missionaries arrived in West Africa and treated the aged bishop with contempt and disdain. He died in 1891 a broken man and his example of both indigenous African mission and a pioneering, cross-culturally sensitive approach to witness to Muslims was swept away and forgotten. We should honour his memory today since, as Andrew Walls says, his Niger Mission 'represents the first sustained missionary engagement with African Islam in modern times'.[7]

---

6. The quotation is reproduced in Andrew Walls, 'Africa as the Theatre of Christian Engagement', p. 145. This article, along with another, 'Samuel Ajayi Crowther (1807–1891)', are both to be found in his *The Cross-Cultural Process in Christian History* (Edinburgh: T&T Clark, 2002) and have been drawn upon in this section.

7. Walls, 'Samuel Ajayi Crowther', p. 161.

Mission, conversion and culture

While both Francis of Assisi and Samuel Crowther provide us with models of peaceful engagement with Islam, motivated by love and given practical expression by wisdom and humility, both men were also absolutely clear that their calling was to bear faithful witness to Christ. In other words, they sought and prayed for the *conversion* of their hearers, recognizing that if they could bring Muslim rulers to recognize Jesus Christ as lord, their evangelism would impact the wider community. Conversion has remained central to the goal of the Christian mission, but it has been understood in many different ways, not all of which have been helpful at the sensitive frontiers where different faiths meet and clash. I want then, in the remainder of this chapter, to consider what biblical conversion actually involves, and how this understanding of conversion may help us in the practice of mission in our troubled world.

The critical turning point in the history of the early church as told in the book of Acts, is the event which has come to be known as the 'Council of Jerusalem'. This meeting was convened as the result of the success of Paul's Gentile mission, which provoked a reaction among Jewish believers in Jesus who wanted to impose the requirements and traditions of the law of Moses on the flood of pagan converts now turning to God. The same issue had arisen earlier when, to his great surprise, Peter had found himself on previously unknown territory in the house of the Roman centurion, Cornelius. Unlike Paul, Peter did not set out to evangelize pagans, but rather found himself – against his will – on the new frontiers of mission where surprises abound and inherited theological presuppositions no longer work. The discovery of 'a large gathering' of Gentiles, all eager 'to listen to everything' God had to say to them (Acts 10:23–33), leaves Peter astonished. However, he learns from this experience and confesses that his previous prejudices had to be abandoned in the light of the discovery that 'God does not show favouritism but *accepts from every nation the one who fears him and does what is right*' (10:34–35). Peter's sermon on this occasion was interrupted by the outpouring of the Holy Spirit, resulting in uncircumcised Gentiles speaking in the tongues of Pentecost and praising God. It is as though God himself intervenes to sweep these people into his kingdom before Peter and his companions can make something other than, or additional to, faith necessary to conversion. Later, when the apostle is arraigned before the Jewish leaders in Jerusalem and sharply criticized for having social contact with the uncircumcised Gentiles, his defence is to say: *God did it!*

By the time we reach Acts 15, the situation has changed in two ways: the conservatism of Jewish believers appears to have hardened, while the number of Gentile converts has swollen into a flood. Peter's Gentile believers could be accommodated by conservative Jews as exceptions to the general rule, but now something of a completely different order is taking place, as Paul and Barnabas report that God has 'opened a door of faith to the Gentiles' (14:27). That is to say, they are now turning to Christ *en masse* in a way which threatens to overturn Jewish practices hallowed by centuries of tradition and apparently authorized by divine revelation. This was, in the language used in modern mission studies, a *paradigm change*, a move across a cultural frontier which seemed to be creating a new way of being Christian. Little wonder then that it provoked such fierce debate.

The crucial turning point in that debate comes with the statement of James, the leader of the Jerusalem church, that 'we should not make it difficult for the Gentiles who are turning to God' (15:19). There is both great wisdom and profound insight in this statement and it contains an implicit warning that the guardians of established traditions of faith may erect *cultural* barriers which become insurmountable obstacles for people from other contexts *who are already being drawn to Christ*. The statement of James can be regarded as the apostolic foundation of a valid cultural *pluralism* within early Christianity; in other words, the New Testament recognizes the authenticity of different cultures, and permits and encourages people to confess and obey the gospel within their own worlds, rather than requiring them to abandon all that is loved and familiar in order to find Christ *in somebody else's cultural world*.

This crucial event in the history of the early church highlights the central place of *conversion* in the Christian mission, but it also provides us with a definition of what this actually means, and clearly distinguishes it from other ways of presenting the claims of Christ at the frontiers between cultures. If the decision taken in Jerusalem involves the acceptance of cultural pluralism within Christianity, it also means that the alternative possibility, of imposing cultural uniformity, *is to be rejected*. Andrew Walls has pointed out the difference between *proselytism*, which is what Jewish believers were arguing for, and *conversion*, which meant turning toward Christ from within the convert's own world and discovering what discipleship would mean from within this new cultural situation. Here is Walls' important description of the distinction between these two ways of doing mission:

> This distinction between the convert and the proselyte is of fundamental importance. If the first Gentile believers had become proselytes, living exactly the lifestyle of those who

brought them to Christ, they might have become very devout
believers, but they would have had virtually no impact on
their society; they would effectively have been taken out of
that society. In fact, it was their task as converts to convert
their society; convert it in the sense that they had to learn
to keep turning their ways of thinking and doing things –
which of course were Greek ways of thinking and doing
things – towards Christ, opening them up to his influence.
In this way a truly Greek, Hellenistic type of Christianity was
able to emerge. Not only so, but that Hellenistic Christianity
was able to penetrate the Hellenistic intellectual and social
heritage.[8]

The central issue which this raises for 'mission in a troubled
world' now becomes clear: do we understand and practice
mission in the light of the apostolic principle that converts
must be encouraged to turn to Christ from within their own
cultural worlds, or have we actually reverted to a form of
proselytization in which one way of being Christian is
imposed on other people, divorcing them from their societies
and so closing down the opportunity for the penetration of
cultures different from our own? I suggest that the verdict
of history is that the radical model which we find in the New
Testament has frequently been ignored, replaced by mission
in an imperialist mode as the conquest and suppression
of other cultural worlds. This has been the case even when
evangelists have used the language of conversion, since
this terminology has frequently been accompanied by the
practice of proselytism, so that 'converts' were required to
accept faith in Christ in precisely the forms in which this was

---

8. Andrew Walls, 'From Christendom to World Christianity', in
   The Cross-Cultural Process in Christian History, p. 68.

already known to the missionaries.[9] The critical issue then becomes whether we can return to the apostolic example today, and what this might mean in practice at the crucial frontiers of our time with both the culture of modernity and economism, on the one hand, and with Islam on the other? What would it mean at these frontiers to heed James' judgment in Jerusalem two thousand years ago, that 'we should not make it difficult' for post-Christian secularists in a globalized world, or for Muslims, whether in Europe or Africa, 'who are turning to God'?

The pathway to the other side

We may recall here the question asked by Theodore von Laue at the end of our first chapter: 'How is it possible to establish common ground with strangers across the barriers of cultural incomprehension and ingrained political hostility? *How can one get to the other side?*' When those words were written in 1987, von Laue was already describing a world in which peoples around the globe were being 'compressed against their will into an inescapable but highly unstable

9. The history of modern missions from the West contains many examples of confusing conversion with proselytism, as the tragic end of Samuel Crowther's life and ministry discussed above shows. However, that churches of African origin have made the same mistake can be seen from the language used by the President of the Pentecostal Fellowship of Nigeria (PFN), who declared in 1993, 'We will take over the whole of Africa'. There is a clear echo of the imperialist model of mission in this statement. See Paul Freston, *Evangelicals and Politics in Asia, Africa and Latin America* (Cambridge: Cambridge University Press, 2001), p. 186.

interdependence laced with explosive tensions'.[10] In the inter-
vening period those tensions have increased as the gulf
between the rich and the poor has widened, millions of
people have become displaced and homeless, and the barriers
between nations, or between people of different ethnic
origins or religious beliefs *within* nations, have grown taller
and more difficult to cross. How is mission to be done in this
troubled and increasingly violent world?

Let me offer in conclusion some principles, or guidelines,
to those who seek the pathway to the other side. *First*, the
'other worlds' which lie beyond the boundaries of culture and
religions are always likely to be places where surprises await
those who come from outside. This was, as we have been
reminded, the experience of the apostle Peter whose preconceptions of Roman pagans were blown away by the
discovery of a centurion who was 'devout and god-fearing'
and whose regular prayers to heaven were clearly heard and
answered. The story of Peter and Cornelius in Acts 10 reminds
us that God is always ahead of us in mission; we do not
introduce him to places and people completely unfamiliar
with his presence and grace, but rather discover in a multitude
of ways evidence of prepared ground in those works of the
Holy Spirit that are not dependent upon us. We noticed above
how Samuel Crowther discovered a Muslim ruler who was
able to say 'amen' to a prayer taken from the Anglican Prayer
Book. But could this also happen the other way round? Might
we find Muslim prayers which breathe the spirit of longing
for fellowship with God, to which *we* could say 'amen'? Here
is such a prayer, taken from a Muslim devotional manual:

---

10. Theodore von Laue, *The World Revolution of Westernization:
    The Twentieth Century in Global Perspective* (New York: Oxford
    University Press, 1987), p. 7.

I have naught but my destitution
   To plead for me with Thee.
And in my poverty I put forward that destitution as my plea.
I have no power save to knock at Thy door,
   And if I be turned away, at what door shall I knock?
Or on whom shall I call, crying his name,
   If Thy generosity is refused to Thy destitute one?
   Far be it from Thy generosity to drive the disobedient one
      to despair!
Generosity is more freehanded, grace wider than that.
In lowly wretchedness I have come to Thy door,
   Knowing that degradation there finds help.
In full abandon I put my trust in Thee,
   Stretching out my hands to Thee, a pleading beggar.[11]

But there is a further lesson to be learned from Peter's mission to Cornelius in that it serves as a reminder that we must not take ourselves too seriously in mission! There is *humour* in this story, and we are meant to smile when we hear the apostle repeatedly confessing his confusion and difficulty in trying to work out just what God was up to! It seems to me that mission has an element of *clowning* about it, and when we recognize our foolish mistakes, both in our preconceptions about God's ways and in our prejudices about other people, we may need simply to laugh at ourselves.

Of course, what we are describing here is what has been called in theological language the *missio Dei* – the 'mission of God'. The tragedy of so much frantic evangelistic activity is that it reduces mission to a human project which we own and control, failing to recognize that we are simply given the

11. Constance Padwick, *Muslim Devotions. A Study of Prayer-Manuals in Common Use* (London: SPCK, 1969), p. 218.

privilege of sharing in a mission initiated by God, and pursued by him in ways which defy human perception or anticipation. We are dependent upon the Lord, but the reverse is not true and, as Paul makes clear to the Romans, we should never forget 'the kindness and sternness of God', because our failure to do mission in a manner reflecting his *kindness*, will expose us (as it did the Jewish people) to the sternness which removes us from his work and finds others who are in tune with God's own heart (Rom. 11:22–23).

The *second* principle of mission for travellers to the 'other side' concerns the importance of an informed and sensitive understanding of the social, historical and religious factors which may have caused a negative reaction to evangelism. I have earlier suggested that we need to ask whether Muslim hostility to Christianity is always a rejection of the gospel, or whether it often expresses a defence against forms of Christianity involving precisely the syncretism with secular modernism which we have heard Lesslie Newbigin denouncing? *Mission never takes place in a historical, cultural vacuum, but is always influenced by factors which often lie hidden from view, such as negative collective memories of disturbing events in the past, or social, political and economic factors which may profoundly influence the perception of those who are the bearers of the message of Christ.* We communicate with words, and what we say and how we say it is supremely important, but the act of communication also involves non-verbal elements which are at least as important as the correct articulation of the message in language. It is possible to say the right things, but to say them with such anger, or arrogance, or with such complete disregard for their reception, that the manner of the presentation drowns out the truth of the message. Or even more seriously, it is possible to speak truly of Christ, the humble, suffering servant, who had 'no place to lay his head', and

for this message to sound completely hollow when brought
by people whose lifestyles display their comfortable and
privileged existence in a world marred by so much poverty
and suffering. It is not only Muslims, but non-Western
Christians who have frequently challenged the way in which
mission has involved the bringing of a whole package in
which the liberating message of the gospel has become fused
with alien cultural elements which threaten to overwhelm and
displace ancient, local traditions.[12] More than thirty years ago,
René Padilla expressed precisely this concern in a message to
the first Lausanne Congress in 1974, which still comes to us
with prophetic power:

> The problem is that one version of culture-Christianity, with
> an inadequate theological foundation and conditioned by

---

12. It is worth recalling that the 1978 Glen Eyrie Report on Muslim
    Evangelization, sponsored by the Lausanne Movement,
    concluded that too many missionaries had 'tended to
    misrepresent and belittle the moral and religious stature of
    Muhammed and the Quran'. At the same time, they were
    'largely indifferent to the task of reducing the mistrust and
    misunderstanding which accentuated past tensions and rivalries'.
    While failing to recognize 'the deterioration of Christian values
    in the Christian world' they openly encouraged 'the process of
    secularization in the Muslim world'. This report, which limited
    its findings to 'the responsibilities of North American Christians
    toward the Muslim world', concluded that, 'We North American
    Christians are only beginning to discover that all too often we
    have preached a westernized, truncated message that does not do
    full justice to the biblical revelation'. See John Stott (ed.), *Making
    Christ Known: Historic Documents From The Lausanne Movement,
    1974–1989* (Grand Rapids: Eerdmans, 1996), pp. 123, 131.

'fierce pragmatism' . . . should be regarded as the official evangelical position and the measure of orthodoxy around the world . . . Under the Spirit of God, each culture has something to contribute in connection with the understanding of the Gospel and its implications for the life and mission of the church. [Western] culture-Christianity should not be allowed to deprive us of the possibility that we all – whatever our race, nationality, language or culture – as equal members in the one body of Christ, 'attain to mature manhood, to the measure of the stature of the fullness of Christ' (Eph. 4:13).[13]

Which brings us, finally, to the *third* principle for those who seek to journey 'to the other side'. In our troubled world we will need to disentangle the good news of Christ from the various cultural wrappers in which it has been contained, but this will only be the prelude to the more challenging task of making the gospel itself available both within the Islamic world *and* to millions of people in the post-Christian West who now belong to a culture which was once, in some sense, 'Christian', but has turned away from faith. All that we have said earlier concerning the frontier with Islam also applies to that other, deeply challenging frontier with unbelief, shaped by the secular-humanist worldview which is now such a fundamentally important element in the world scene. At this frontier too there is need for real understanding of the causes

13. René Padilla, 'Evangelism and the World', in J. D. Douglas (ed.), *Let The Earth Hear His Voice. International Congress on World Evangelization, Lausanne, Switzerland* (Minneapolis: World Wide Publications, 1975), pp. 140–141. I have changed one word in this quotation: Padilla spoke of 'American culture-Christianity' and I have preferred to describe this more broadly, and consistent with the critique of Newbigin earlier in these studies, as 'Western'.

of the choices made by people who have consciously abandoned faith, as well as the sense of alienation of later generations who live with the personal and social consequences of secularism, even as they confess, like young people in post-Communist Eastern Europe, that 'We have forgotten that we have forgotten God'![14] However, those who move across this frontier and offer true and faithful friendship to people 'on the other side', will also discover that the God whose very existence may be denied *is not absent from this territory.* Here too we may meet our 'Cornelius's' whose pursuit of love and passion for justice may put us to shame and undermine many of our preconceptions. And here too, the recognition of the factors which led to the rejection of Christianity will need to be carefully explored and sympathetically understood. Only then can the task of 'translating' the message of the gospel afresh for the world we have described begin – and to that task we turn in the next chapter.

14. A former student of mine, Mike Edwards, reported this statement made by secular young people in conversation with a group of their Christian peers in an eastern German city. The dialogue concerned issues related to identity, meaning and moral values and it resulted in surprising discoveries for the young believers who made the journey from the church to 'the other side'.

4

Translating the gospel for the globalized world of the twenty-first century

We have seen in our previous study that the 'apostles and elders' who met at the Council of Jerusalem recognized that conversion, not proselytism, was to be the normative practice in Christian mission. That momentous decision meant that cultural pluralism was recognized from the beginning as valid; more than that, it was to be the way in which the richness and glory of God's grace in Christ might be discovered and displayed within the world. This principle was of absolutely fundamental importance in the ministry of Paul, becoming an issue which brought him into conflict with a variety of opponents who wished to revert to the proselytizing model, and providing the foundation for his great vision of the ultimate goal of mission. Nowhere perhaps, is this vision more clearly stated than in the great prayer in the letter to the Ephesians, in which we hear the petition that believers may have the power, *together with all the Lord's holy people*, to grasp how wide and long and high and deep is the love of Christ' (Eph. 3:18–19). The phrase 'all the Lord's holy people' (or 'saints' in older versions) does not refer to a collection of disparate individuals, but rather, as the previous discussion of the reconciliation of Jews and Gentiles within the one body of Christ makes clear, it anticipates the contributions to the knowledge of the surpassing love of Christ to be made by saints from all *nations* and from every *culture*. For Paul, the previously hidden purpose of God, to destroy the barriers, what he calls 'the dividing wall of hostility', between races, has been revealed as the direct outcome of mission, through which both Jews and Gentiles have found in the crucified Christ reconciliation, healing, and personal and social peace.

It is this great vision which drives Paul on, so that he informs believers in Rome that he feels obligated to preach Christ both to 'Greeks and non-Greeks, both to the wise and the foolish' (Rom. 1:14), so that people from every nation may hear the good news and, having embraced it, share from their unique perspectives what this indescribable love means to them. Indeed, before the end of the letter to the Romans we are suddenly informed that the apostle's real objective in wanting to come to the imperial capital, is that this might be the staging post for mission to the very ends of the earth. Thus, he tells the hearers of the letter, who may well have been nonplussed by this revelation: 'I will go to Spain and visit you on the way' (Rom. 15:28). Commentators on the letter to the Romans have not paid much attention to the significance of this missionary vision with regard to the purpose and meaning of the epistle as a whole, but as Robert Jewett has recently shown, the letter was 'designed to prepare the ground for the complicated project of the Spanish mission'. Paul was determined that the population of Spain, at the very margins of the empire, and from Rome's perspective people without status or honour, the ultimate barbarians, should know of the surpassing love of Christ. Paul's mission included,

. . . the insistence that the impartial righteousness of God does not discriminate against 'barbarians' such as the Spaniards, that all claims to cultural superiority are false, that imperial propaganda must be recognized as bogus, and that the domineering behaviour of congregations toward one another must be overcome if the missional hope to unify the world in praise of God is to be fulfilled.[1]

Translating the message of the gospel

What we observe taking place within the period of the New Testament is the first missionary translation of the gospel of Jesus Christ as that message is taken across the frontier which divided the Jewish and Gentile worlds. The difficulty of this task is reflected in Paul's request at the end of the Colossian letter (4:3), repeated in the Ephesian correspondence, asking his hearers to pray for him that 'whenever I speak, words may be given me so that I will fearlessly make known the mystery of the gospel' (Eph. 6:19). Concealed within this apparently simple statement we can detect the struggle and anguish which accompanies cross-cultural missionary communication. It involves an endless search for the right words, for language which is clear, faithful and accurate. The text suggests that Paul is well aware of the slippery, ambiguous nature of human tongues, so that words which in one setting may have communicated the meaning of the gospel directly and powerfully, in another can distort and misrepresent it.

---

1. Robert Jewett, *Romans. A Commentary*, Hermeneia (Minneapolis: Fortress Press, 2007), p. 79. This magnificent commentary places Paul's mission squarely at the heart of the purpose and meaning of the letter and greatly illuminates the historical and socio-political context of Paul's ministry.

Words which originally were dynamic can grow stale and old through overuse and over-familiarity, becoming mere jargon and devoid of the power to transform people. Thus, one aspect of communication involves the search for *clarity*, for language that avoids mystification and makes the good news clear and arresting to ordinary people.

However, there is a danger at the opposite end of the spectrum, and this involves the cheapening of the gospel; the choice of language which empties the message of its glory and transcendent value. This is reflected in Paul's description of the good news as a *mystery*, a term which is itself an example of contextualization in that it refers to the Greek mystery religions which were a significant aspect of the culture of the ancient world. The application of this term to the gospel means that Paul is dismissing the claims of the Greek religions to involve 'mysteries'; those initiation ceremonies which took place in secluded temples in the dead of night and involved spectacular events which were claimed to be revelations from the gods, were false and empty! The real mystery is that God has become flesh and dwelt among us, that in a person of flesh and blood the very life of the eternal has been displayed within human history, and that this revelation of divine love and justice so exposed the corruption of the powers which govern the world that it resulted in the humiliation and death of the Son of God. *That is the ultimate mystery, and no human language can ever do it justice.* Thus, Paul, like all missionary preachers who follow him, faces the difficult tension between the need for clarity in sharing the gospel, on the one hand, and the equally important concern never to devalue the glory of the incarnation of God, on the other.

There is, however, a final thing to be said about Paul's understanding of communication as suggested by this text. Twice he requests prayer that his witness may be *fearless* (Eph. 6:19–20).

Does this suggest that he knows the reality of the temptation to modify the content of the message, to soft-peddle certain aspects of it which are likely to bring a negative reaction from his hearers? Paul is, as he reminds us, 'an ambassador in chains' (6:20), so that his ministry has already resulted in imprisonment, suffering, and the threat of execution. There were clearly aspects of the message of the crucified and risen Messiah which stirred violent opposition, both from conservative Jewish hearers, and from the imperial authorities, to whom the claim that a rabbi nailed to Roman cross was the true Saviour and Lord of the whole earth was both ridiculous and seditious. Does this explain the double request for the prayers of his hearers that his communication of Christ will be *fearless*? And does this also serve as a reminder to us that any genuine preaching of the gospel will have a prophetic edge which will disturb and alarm those who are privileged and powerful? We may indeed ask ourselves whether the syncretism we have discussed earlier, the creation of various forms of culture-Christianity in which the cutting edge of the gospel is blunted by its accommodation to the spirit of the age, may have been a way of avoiding the demanding path of faithful mission which requires a willingness to suffer and die for Christ.[2]

---

2. It is worth noting here that had Paul managed to realize his ambition to reach Spain with the gospel, he would have faced the biggest linguistic challenge of his life. Greek was not widely known there and Latin was used in the urban areas under Roman control. However, beyond these footholds of colonial power 'the Celt-Iberian and other languages continued to be spoken by most of the population'. Jewett concludes: 'For the first time in Christian history, as far as we know, a two-step process of translation was required: from Greek to Latin and then into various local languages', *Romans*, p. 88.

Contextualization, Islam and the free market

The apostolic model of mission we have described here means that, in a unique way, Christianity is a *translatable faith*. It is not tied to a single culture or language, nor does it depend on one, sacred geographical centre. Jerusalem does not mean for Christians what Mecca means for Muslims. The history of this tradition during the past two thousand years has been marked by repeated acts of cross-cultural transmission through which the gospel became embedded within many cultures and expressed in different languages. Indeed, in recent studies of the history of mission, a series of major turning points have been identified, commencing with the first great missionary movement associated with Paul, in which the faith has crossed cultural barriers and has been embraced by peoples who received Christ as the saviour of their worlds. What makes the present time so significant is that we appear to be living through the latest of these transitions as the long era of Western Christendom has given way to a new situation in which churches across the Global South take up the baton passed to them during the previous two hundred years. Andrew Walls, referring to the discussion of the uniting of Jew and Gentile within the one body of Christ in Ephesians 2, has said that the 'Ephesian moment', which all too briefly united two separate peoples, thus displaying the power of the gospel to bring about unity-in-diversity – *that 'moment' has come again in the twenty-first century, only now it brings the possibility of an expression of faith uniting people from many cultures in a way that will be richer and more significant 'than has ever happened since the first century'.*[3]

---

3. Andrew Walls, 'The Ephesian Moment', in *The Cross-Cultural Process in Christian History* (Edinburgh: T&T Clark, 2002), p. 78.

There is, however, a significantly new and unprecedented dimension in the context for mission in the world of today: it is the phenomenon which goes by the name of *globalization*. This term is related to the ideology of the free market which we have discussed earlier in these studies, and it also suggests the completion of what Theodore von Laue describes as the 'world revolution of Westernization'. It is not possible to provide a detailed description and analysis of globalization here, but it is vital to notice that this term signifies something more than simply a theory of economics.[4] It represents an ideology, a worldview, and is presented by its powerful advocates and beneficiaries as offering a global culture which will eventually bring wealth and abundance to the entire human race. There are clear echoes here of the claims made for the Roman Empire during the period of the New Testament, claims which were challenged and repudiated by the first Christians who detected signs of idolatry and blasphemy in Roman propaganda. What we face today is, I suggest, even more sinister and challenging, because of its dehumanizing tendencies, its failed promises and its global spread. Describing the impact of this culture on traditional societies and religions, Jeremy Seabrook notes, 'Unlike the resistance which developed to earlier occupying powers, it is

---

4. See Daniel Groody, *Globalization, Spirituality and Justice.*
   Navigating the Path to Peace (New York: Orbis Books, 2007); and
   the many studies of Zygmunt Bauman, including *Globalization:*
   The Human Consequences (Cambridge: Polity Press, 1998); *Liquid*
   Times: Living in an Age of Uncertainty (Cambridge: Polity Press,
   2007); *Wasted Lives: Modernity and its Outcasts* (Cambridge: Polity
   Press, 2004). The impact of globalization on cities is discussed by
   Saskia Sassen in *Globalization and Its Discontents* (New York: The
   New Press, 1998).

harder to set up a liberation movement or a freedom struggle, since the adversaries are impalpable, dissolving and regrouping all the time, the better to take the citadels of faith and custom from within.'[5]

That warning about the threat which globalization presents to 'faith and custom from within' is extremely pertinent to this discussion, and it alerts us to the possibility that the growth of Christianity in so many areas of the Global South may prove to be very short-lived unless believers in Africa, Asia and Latin America can find the spiritual and theological resources with which to resist and challenge this ideology. Or, to express this in missiological language, how can we contextualize the gospel in relation to the culture of globalization?

Let me suggest three areas in which biblical and theological reflection is urgently required at this most pressing of contemporary frontiers. *First*, the most fundamental need relates to *the biblical revelation of God*. You may recall that in our first study we noticed the way in which modern economic theory, while denying God any role in the operations of the modern market system, actually took over what had previously been regarded as divine attributes and transferred them to earth. The market now became omnipotent, infallible and beyond challenge. In our times, with the collapse of Communism, the claims made for the market have become ever more extended and universal. Where human beings previously bowed before God's sovereign power, now they are required to acknowledge the dominance of the laws of the market and to submit to this pervasive, mysterious and often unpredictable power. Christians have of course protested at the

---

5. Jeremy Seabrook, *Consuming Cultures: Globalization and Local Lives* (Oxford: New Internationalist Publications, 2004), p. 24.

exclusion of God from the modern worldview, but they have rarely faced up to a far deeper and more disturbing issue; namely, the question of whether the image of God in Christendom, which presented the deity largely in terms of *power*, was ever true to the revelation given to the prophets of Israel and supremely through Christ? Douglas Meeks, whose work we referred to earlier, has suggested that the God of the Bible, far from being disconnected from the economic realm, may actually be described in economic language as the supreme provider and carer of the earth and all its inhabitants. In God's economy, he writes, human beings are separated from the rest of creation only by the fact that they are mandated 'to keep God's household. Being human is an economic commission to join God the Economist in distributing righteousness so that the world may live'. In language which serves to remind us that the faith of the Bible is far closer to the primal worldview of traditional Africa than it is to the secularized West, Meeks observes that in Scripture to be human means possessing 'a right to a life-giving share of the world's resources so that one can serve God's life-giving economy for the creation'.[6]

---

6. M. Douglas Meeks, *God the Economist: The Doctrine of God and Political Economy* (Minneapolis: Fortress Press, 1989), pp. 90–91. See too the comment of Bob Goudzwaard: 'Somehow in our modern arrogance we have missed the wisdom of ancient Israel, whose economy was an economy of abundance (*shalom*) and inclusion on the basis of limited means. In contrast, ours is an economy of scarcity and exclusion on the basis of an ever-expanding flow of means', 'Economic Growth: is more always better?', in Donald Hay and Alan Kreider (eds.), *Christianity and the Culture of Economics* (Cardiff: University of Wales Press, 2001), p. 161.

The doctrine of God is thus of crucial importance at the missionary frontier with the ideology of the free market. But it is no less significant with regard to the dialogue with Islam, precisely because within this tradition God *never was divorced from the spheres of economics and politics.* It is precisely Islam's insistence that the whole of life, including the economic dimension, must be brought under the ethical control of divine law which is a major cause of the tension between this faith and the secular worldview of the modern West which excludes the sacred from the public square and confines God to the private world of the family and the home. The recovery of the biblical understanding of God, the God who breaks into history to set the captives free, and who in Christ brings his alternative reign of justice and righteousness to a broken and divided world, is an absolute precondition for any meaningful engagement with Muslims. In this context the Lord's Prayer, with its pleading that the kingdom may come, and the will of God be done *'on earth as it is in heaven'* can never be an empty liturgical statement, but rather takes us to the heart of mission, even as it reminds us of the true nature of Yahweh.

The *second* area in which theological foundations need to be laid for mission to our troubled world, concerns *the nature and scope of the good news of the gospel.* If it is indeed true that we stand today at a juncture in history at which the Christian traditions received from the West are growing old and seem increasingly unable to bridge the gap between the church and the world, then the missiological challenge before us must include the task of undertaking the latest translation of the message of the gospel, by means of which it might really come as good news to the world of the twenty-first century. Lesslie Newbigin pointed out that almost all missiological writing dealing with the subject of contextualization was focused on a one-way process in which the gospel, assumed to be culture-free, was transmitted into the many cultures of Africa, Asia and Latin America. The problem with this, he argued, was that the entire endeavour overlooked 'the most widespread, powerful and persuasive among all contemporary cultures', namely the globalized, modern, Western culture which we have discussed. Newbigin concluded that 'there is no higher priority for the research work of missiologists than to ask the question of *what would be involved in a genuinely missionary encounter between the gospel and this modern Western culture*'.[7]

But perhaps there is a prior question which needs to be answered before the difficult work of translation can take place, namely, *do we first need to recover the fullness of the gospel itself?* Certainly, those of us who have been socialized into ways of thinking which simply take for granted the individualism that dominates the Western way of life must engage in a process of critical self-examination in which we ask whether our cultural context has created distorting lenses through which we have read the Bible. Fortunately, it is precisely the arrival of World Christianity which can assist us in this process, since to an extent which is unprecedented, all of us are now able to enlist the help of believers outside our own cultures who can identify our cultural biases and blind spots. As the Hispanic theologian Justo González has observed, the demise of Christendom and the dramatic growth of World Christianity is creating a situation in which the whole body of Christ may be led together into a deeper understanding of the biblical message. González is worth quoting at length on this subject:

---

7. Lesslie Newbigin, in Paul Weston (ed.), *Lesslie Newbigin: Missionary Theologian. A Reader* (London: SPCK, 2006), p. 108, emphasis added.

The meaning of the Exodus and of the law that springs from it is best understood by those who have an experience of slavery and a long trek through the wilderness. The minority report of the prophets is best understood by those who are not usually included in the chronicles of the kings or of high society. The exile is best understood by those who live in societies that are not theirs, and who 'by the rivers of Babylon' are called upon to sing the songs of the Lord in a foreign land. The enormity of the self-marginalization of God in Galilee is best understood by modern-day outsiders in modern-day Galilees – ghettos, barrios, and the misdeveloped countries.[8]

Referring to Martin Luther's famous distinction between a 'theology of glory' and a 'theology of the cross', the one perceiving God in terms of power, prestige and success, while the other identifies him with suffering, weakness and loss, González concludes that with the end of Christendom the theology of glory which accompanied it now represents a 'dying age', and that, in what he calls a 'new Reformation' on a global scale, the worldwide body of Christ is being gifted an opportunity for renewed and greater faithfulness.

The *third* concern for theology at the missionary frontiers we have discussed relates to the nature of the Christian movement itself, or to the character of the *ekklēsia*. What will the church look like in the twenty-first century? I ask this question not simply with regard to existing structures and organizations, but in respect of new movements which may emerge as the outcome of the successful translation of the gospel across the key frontiers which we have discussed in these studies. If those young Germans who had 'forgotten

---

8. Justo González, *Mañana: Christian Theology from a Hispanic Perspective* (Nashville: Abingdon Press, 1990), pp. 49–50.

that they had forgotten God' come, out of their sense of loss, of alienation and the lack of purpose in human existence, to find in Jesus a liberation that restores and renews them, bringing them into the experience of the fullness of life, *what kind of believing community would they form?* Or again, if the person of Jesus, who is by no means unfamiliar to Muslims, were to attract the devotion of more and more young people within this tradition (as is already happening in parts of the Muslim world), would they abandon their religion to identify with existing churches, *or can we envisage the House of Islam being transformed from within?* These questions, stated in this way, may seem radical, but I suggest they are, in fact, merely logical issues arising from the distinction between proselytism and conversion which we have discussed earlier. If our mission involves crossing the contemporary cultural frontiers which have concerned us in these studies to plant the seed of the gospel in a way that leads to conversion, then we cannot require or expect that either modern secular people or devout Muslims will become Christians in the way that we are. The biblical principle that conversion means turning to Christ, and following him *within the convert's existing cultural world*, prevents us from requiring people to abandon that world. Conversion is not about changing one's religion, it is about becoming a disciple of Jesus and following him, perhaps at great cost, within the society or culture which is familiar, cherished and loved. Can we make the leap of imagination required to recognize that both postmodern, secular people, wearied by the spiritual desert which is the modern world of economism, and Muslims, asking deep questions within their own tradition in the light of its encounter with modernity, may have entirely fresh light to share with us on the meaning of Christ were they to be grasped by his redemptive love and, from *within* their socio-cultural worlds, confess him as Lord?[9] It is, I suggest, as we reflect on these issues that the real contours of the still-emerging fresh paradigm of mission for a globalized world begins to take shape.[10]

---

9. An illustration of the 'deep questions' being asked within Islam as the result of its encounter with modernity is provided by Abdullahi Ahmed An-Na'im's *Toward an Islamic Reformation: Civil Liberties, Human Rights, and International Law* (Syracuse: Syracuse University Press, 1996). An-Naim draws upon the work of his teacher, Mahmoud Muhamed Taha, who was executed in Sudan for his views. Both men argue that the core message of Islam is to be located in the early revelations granted to Muhammed, which stress 'the inherent dignity of all human beings, regardless of gender, religious belief, race, and so forth' and insist upon 'complete freedom of choice in matters of religion and faith', ibid., p. 52. For a range of Muslim responses to modernity see John Cooper, Ronald Nettler and Mohamed Mahmood (eds.), *Islam and Modernity: Muslim Intellectuals Respond* (London: I. B. Tauris, 2000). The best general overview of Islam and the modern West known to me is John Esposito's *The Islamic Threat: Myth or Reality?* (3rd edn, New York: Oxford University Press, 1999).

10. Kenneth Cragg is well known as one of the most informed and helpful Christian students of Islam. In a small book published in 1998 he addressed the contemporary challenge of both missionary frontiers which concern us here. He describes Christian mission as in crisis, partly because of 'the irreducible "thereness" of plural religions in the life and story of the world'. The form of mission which seemed possible in 1910, in which Christianity would *replace* other faiths around the world, no longer makes sense in a world where other religions have revived and gained a global presence. Cragg concludes, '"Go ye into all the world" means more than a travel agency. It means going into

Reading the Bible in a globalized world

Throughout the history of Christianity different biblical texts have come into prominence and have shaped the underlying vision and practice of mission at different times. During the modern period William Carey's insistence that the Great Commission at the end of Matthew's Gospel was binding upon Christians in every age resulted in that passage becoming the 'favoured text' in Protestant mission and it has exercised an immense influence over the movement for two hundred years. With the passing of the modern paradigm of mission the question has been asked in recent times as to which texts might be recognized as providing direction for the new era now opening up before a global church. We suggest that no single text can be adequate in this context and that what is, in fact, demanded is a deeper rootedness in the vision and theology of mission which pervades the entire Bible. However, the task of discerning this theology will demand two things: first, a willingness to examine critically what we, and those who have gone before us, have believed the Bible to be saying with regard to the Christian mission, alert to the possibility that negative cultural influences of the kind discussed earlier may have resulted in serious *misreadings* of Scripture. There are, sadly, well-known examples of the manner in which the Bible has been used ideologically to support an unjust and oppressive status quo, so blunting the text's prophetic cutting

---

the heart of cultures and the depths of creeds and codes as well as into the width of the world'. The context in which we now find ourselves may suggest that 'the long, arduous, and patient experience of mission leads us back to where it all began in the meaning of the incarnation . . . ', *The Secular Experience of God* (Leominster: Gracewing, 1998), pp. 63, 74.

edge. In the chapter which follows we shall explore some of the ways in which this has happened in European history.

Second, we will also need a genuine openness to new readings of Scripture, especially those offered to us by believers whose historical, social and cultural contexts are different from ours. The conviction of John Robinson, the pastor of the Pilgrim Fathers on the brink of their momentous trans-Atlantic voyage to the 'new world' of America in 1620, that the rigid traditionalism of the heirs of the Reformation was 'a misery much to be lamented', and that the Lord had 'yet more truth and light to break forth from his holy word', is one we must share in a century in which World Christianity will reshape and reinvigorate the traditions it has inherited. John Robinson anticipated that the widening geographical horizons of the 'new world' would pose fresh questions and open up new insights , so that – as at the beginning – mission would expand and enrich the knowledge of Christ's immense and surpassing love. In the globalized world of the twenty-first century the growth of Christianity in a multiplicity of social and cultural contexts promises to create similar spaces within which fresh light will be shed on the meaning of Christ and his gospel.[11]

---

11. The significance of the cultural shifts which have concerned us here with regard to the theology and practice of mission are discussed in detail in Paul Hiebert's *Missiological Implications of Epistemological Shifts: Affirming Truth in a Modern/Postmodern World* (Harrisburg: Trinity Press International, 1999). He concludes that 'the global church must become an international hermeneutical community in which Christian leaders from around the world become partners in hermeneutics – seeking to understand Scripture under the guidance of the Holy Spirit, to help one another in dealing with the problems they face in their particular contexts, and to check one another's cultural biases', p. 113.

Far from being apprehensive about such a prospect, it should be recognized as the fulfilment of the apostolic vision that mission among the nations would bring into being a multi-cultural church in which 'we all reach unity in the faith and in the knowledge of the Son of God, and become mature, *attaining to the full measure of the fullness of Christ*' (Eph. 4:13). Quite clearly this had not happened when these words were written; it was (and remains) the object of faith, anticipated as a goal yet to be reached. Nonetheless, the emergence of World Christianity in the era of globalization suggests that this apostolic hope may be closer to realization than ever before, and as we 'speak the truth in love' to each other, we may, together, 'in all things grow up into him who is the Head, that is Christ' (4:15).

In the penultimate chapter of this book I wish to suggest that one New Testament document in particular may be about to play a key role in shaping the church's understanding of its mission in this new world. There are clear indications that Paul's letter to the Romans is once again being read with new eyes and in ways that connect the apostle's articulation of the gospel to the specific context of the postmodern, globalized world we have tried to describe. Romans is being heard today as speaking powerfully concerning mission in our globalized, economistic, urban world, precisely because greater attention is being paid than ever before to the original context of the letter and its first hearers. In this process close parallels are emerging between that context and the one which we face today. There are as yet hidden treasures to be discovered, or re-appropriated, within this letter as God, yet again, 'breaks forth more light' from his word, providing guidance, encouragement and inspiration for the missionary calling of a global church in the twenty-first century.

PART 2:
RELEASING THE MESSAGE OF THE BIBLE FOR A DIVIDED CHURCH AND A TROUBLED WORLD

The Bible and globalization: critical reflections on biblical hermeneutics

The year 1492 witnessed developments in European history which marked the beginning of a new epoch. Before dawn one morning in early August, Christopher Columbus and his fellow sailors knelt on a beach in the Spanish port of Palos to confess their sins and receive absolution and the sacrament before setting sail toward unknown western seas. As the sun rose, three vessels, led by the *Santa Maria*, began an epic voyage which was to result in the discovery of what came to be known as the 'New World'. While this event is often remembered, the broader religious context in which it occurred is often overlooked. As James Reston notes in his brilliant study of this period, when Columbus travelled from Granada to Palos, 'the roads must have been clogged with Jews departing Spain, scattering across sea and border in response to the Edict of Expulsion of Ferdinand and Isabella and their Inquisition'.[1] In fact, the deadline set by

---

1. James Reston Jr, *Dogs of God: Columbus, The Inquisition, and the Defeat of the Moors* (London: Faber and Faber, 2006), p. xviii.

the Spanish monarchs for the expulsion of all Jews from their domains was the day after Columbus set sail, so that the event which was to trigger the expansion of European power was inseparable from the *Reconquista* and the brutal expulsion of Sephardic Jews from Spain. At the same time, the conflict between Spanish Catholicism and Islam was understood in apocalyptic terms as a battle which would usher in a new golden age, and Columbus himself conceived of his adventure as likely to add glory to the anticipated triumph of Christian power within and beyond Europe. These events were thus viewed as possessing cosmic significance, as the reconquest and purification of Spain combined with the discovery of new worlds to make possible an age of unprecedented glory. In Reston's words, 'In the cosmic drama, Discovery must join with Reconquest and Purification. Together, the three fitted into the new heaven and earth that was promised in the book of Revelation'.[2]

The mention of the book of Revelation compels us to ask how the Bible was understood in this period and what part was played by particular traditions of interpretation in the epochal events which shaped the world we have inherited? To answer this question we must go back to the twelfth century and the extraordinary visions of the medieval mystic, Joachim of Fiore (1145–1202). After years of profound meditation on the Bible, and frustrated that the gospel seemed not to have brought the blessings promised by the Hebrew prophets, Joachim came to believe that the Revelation of John anticipated a time of future glory, an 'Age of the Spirit', which would be characterized by 'love, joy and freedom, when the knowledge of God would be revealed directly in the hearts of

---

2. Ibid., p. 221.

all men'.[3] The impact of this vision of the 'Third Age' was immense and can be traced through the entire Middle Ages and into the present. Norman Cohn even suggests that the three stages of social history in Marxist theory and the phrase 'The Third Reich' would have had little emotional power had not Joachim's vision of a third age 'entered the common stock of European social mythology'.[4]

The vision of Joachim was to have a profound influence on various movements across Europe, including in Spain at the time of the *Reconquista* at the end of the fifteenth century. The letters of Christopher Columbus make explicit references to the visions of Joachim of Fiore and reveal the profoundly religious motivation of the trans-Atlantic crossings. Thus, during his third voyage in 1498, Columbus wrote:

> I was certain that all would be accomplished, since in truth, 'all things pass away but the word of God will never pass away', the word which has spoken so clearly of these lands by the mouth of Isaiah in so many places in Holy Scripture,

3. Norman Cohn, *The Pursuit of the Millennium: Revolutionary Millenarians and Mystical Anarchists of the Middle Ages* (London: Paladin Books, 1970), p. 108.

4. Ibid., p. 109. In 2005 Ilan Volkov and the BBC Scottish Symphony Orchestra recorded Leoš Janáček's little-known work, 'The Eternal Gospel'. Based on a Czech poem, the text describes Joachim of Fiore announcing the coming of the Spirit's kingdom: 'When affluence and worldly goods and riches/gold, jewels, all shall turn to dust/When every pauper shall be rich in spirit/and all the world inherits eternal Spring.' See the essay by Nigel Simeone in the booklet accompanying this disc, Hyperion Records CDA 67517.

affirming that it is from Spain that the spread of God's Holy Name will go forth . . . '[5]

Two years later, as he prepared to cross the ocean yet again, Columbus linked the expansion of European, and specifically Spanish, power with the eschatological vision at the end of the Bible, stating, 'I am making myself the messenger of the new heaven and the new earth of which our Lord speaks in the Apocalypse by the mouth of St. John . . . '. However, side by side with this religious conviction, we discover language concerning the quest for gold and the taking of slaves which indicate that biblical ideas were completely interwoven with the political and economic objectives of Spain. In the letter cited above, Columbus's assertion of biblical authority is immediately followed by the statement that, ' . . . in the name of the Holy Trinity one could send as many slaves as one could sell', and each of these people taken captive in the New World would be 'worth three [African] blacks'.

The views expressed by Columbus reflected the worldview he shared with his compatriots at the time. Ferdinand and Isabella, it came to be believed, were to play a crucial role in European sacred history, being destined to complete the evangelization of Europe, recover the Holy Land, and become the agents for the triumph of Christ to the very ends of the earth. Ferdinand himself believed that he possessed a divine destiny which involved purifying the Catholic faith of heresy, driving the Muslims from Spain, and recovering the City of David as a prelude to the return of Christ.

However, if the epochal events in Spain during the last decades of the fifteenth century seemed to their beneficiaries

---

5. Jean Comby, *How To Understand the History of Christian Mission* (London: SCM Press, 1996), p. 60.

to be the harbingers of the final triumph of Christendom and the fulfilments of biblical prophecies of an age of glory, their consequences for minority groups within Europe and, even more, for the millions of indigenous peoples on the receiving end of the Spanish missions, were very different. Writing on the occasion of the five-hundredth anniversary of the expeditions of Columbus, the Chilean theologian Pablo Richard described 1492 as the year in which *death* came to the 'New World'. It has been estimated that when Europeans first set foot on the shores of South America, the indigenous population was 100 million people, yet less than a century later, by 1570, it had fallen to between ten to twelve million. Richard argues that this 'was the greatest genocide in the history of humanity' and it was tragically underpinned by a theological justification which subordinated the biblical tradition 'to the historical rationality of the conquest'.[6] Thus, the Spanish theologian Juan Sepulveda applied the Just War tradition to the conquest of the Americas, defending the use of violence in the evangelization of uncivilized and 'barbarian' peoples, and concluding that it was 'thanks to terror combined with preaching' that the native peoples 'received the Christian religion'.[7]

Reading the Bible from the perspective of the victims

Within half a century of the arrival of the Spanish *conquistadores* new Catholic missionaries crossed the ocean to South

---

6. Pablo Richard, '1492: The Violence of God and the Future of Christianity', in Leonardo Boff and Virgil Elizondo (eds.), *1492–1991: The Voice of the Victims* (London: SCM Press, 1990), pp. 59, 61. See in this same volume, Enrique Dussel, 'The Real Motives for the Conquest', pp. 30–46.

7. Richard, '1492', p. 63.

America, among whom were men who reacted with utter dismay at the discovery of the treatment meted out to the indigenous populations under the pretence of evangelism. As the terrible reality of the 'conquest' began to sink in, voices were raised in prophetic protest against the oppression of the native peoples and the subversion of the gospel of Christ which made this possible. The protestors had 'read and re-read the Bible' and concluded that what they were witnessing amounted to an oppression 'much greater than that suffered by the people of God in Egypt or Babylon, or even by the primitive church under Roman oppression'. In other words, they were witnesses to an historic injustice which 'leaped over the boundaries of the Bible!'.[8] For example, in 1511 Antonio de Montesinos preached a passionate and uncompromising sermon on the island of Hispaniola (modern Haiti), denouncing the Spanish for having obliterated a beautiful culture and turned a paradise into a desert. He posed a series of searching questions which climaxed with the insistence that anyone claiming to follow Christ was obligated to love his neighbour (in this case, the aboriginal people) as himself. Seated in the dumbstruck congregation was a young missionary priest, recently arrived from Spain on a ship which was part of the largest Spanish fleet ever to cross the Atlantic Ocean. His name was Bartolomé des Las Casas and three years later, having witnessed at first hand the massacre of native people on Cuba, he experienced a radical conversion which led him to conclude that 'everything that was done to the Indians . . . was unjust and tyrannical'.[9]

---

8. Maximilian Salinas, 'The Voices of Those Who Spoke Up For the Victims', in Boff and Elizondo (eds.), *Voice of the Victims*, p. 105.

9. Bartolomé des Las Casas, *A Short Account of the Destruction of the Indies* (Harmondsworth: Penguin Books, 1992), p. xxii.

Las Casas has left us with a classic account of what he called
the 'destruction of the Indies', providing a chilling eye-witness
description of the genocide, while also revealing the concern
he shared with all the prophetic opponents of the *conquistadores* that, unless there was repentance on the part of the
privileged and powerful in Spain, that nation would itself be
destroyed 'for sins against the honour of God and the True
Faith'.[10] Justo González has commented on the fact that two
completely contrasting readings of the Bible emerged from a
single theological tradition:

> One simply continued the ideology that had been developed
> around the *Reconquista* against the Moors, which saw Spain
> as having a divinely appointed task to take the land from the
> infidel and establish orthodox, Catholic Christianity. The
> other, while sharing most of the theological tradition with the
> former, *reversed that ideology, calling Spain and her representatives
> to repentance.*[11]

González asks how such 'voices of compassion' could have
emerged from within the context of Inquisition, reconquest

10. Ibid., p. 127. Las Casas' s book was quickly translated into French
and Dutch and was published in an English version in 1583.
J. H. Elliott points out that its circulation throughout Europe
coincided with increased tensions between Catholic Spain and
the nations of northern Europe, while the conflict 'between
Rome and Geneva was approaching its climax', *The Old World
and the New – 1492–1650* (Cambridge: Cambridge University
Press, 1992), p. 95.

11. Justo González, 'Voices of Compassion Yesterday and Today',
in Guillermo Cook (ed.), *New Face of the Church in Latin America*
(New York: Orbis Books, 1994), p. 11, emphasis added.

and colonial expansion? How did a radically alternative reading of the Bible come about which both critiqued 'the nation's greatest moment in history', and provided a counter-cultural, theological analysis of what was happening? His answer, which we shall need to remember when we come to consider the role of the Bible in the context of full-blown globalization, is that the 'voices of compassion' belonged to people who had 'heard a different Voice' as they shared their lives 'in solidarity with the oppressed natives of these lands'.

By the middle of the sixteenth century, and in the wake of the Reformation, the missionary impulse which had accompanied Spanish Catholic expansion appeared among French Protestants. The story of Jean de Léry and the attempt of a group of French Reformed pastors to gain a foothold in Brazil is little known, but it demonstrates again how different readings of the Bible can emerge within a single theological tradition. In 1556 Léry and his companions set sail from the French port of Honfleur in response to a letter addressed to John Calvin in Geneva requesting that the Reformed church send people 'well instructed in the Christian religion' to Brazil. We are fortunate that Léry was both a careful observer with a sharp eye for detail, and an excellent writer, so that his book, *A History of a Voyage to the Land Called Brazil, Otherwise Called America* (1580) is an invaluable historical source and a neglected classic of missionary literature.[12] Léry and his fellow missionaries attempted to work among the Tupinamba Indians but their encounter with this completely new cultural world led to radically different opinions concerning the moral and spiritual condition of this

---

12. Jean de Léry's *History of a Voyage To The Land Called Brazil, Otherwise Called America* was translated into English by Janet Whatley, who also provides an excellent introduction (Berkeley: University of California Press, 1990).

primal people. On the one hand, the leader of the group reported back to Calvin in Geneva that the indigenous people were of 'such a stupid mind that they make no distinction between right and wrong' and did not even know that God existed. By contrast, Léry, having immersed himself in the culture in a manner that anticipated much later methods of research in social anthropology, reached a very different view. The Tupi, he wrote, have 'little care or worry for the things of this world' and do not 'drink of those murky, pestilential springs, from which flow so many streams of distrust, avarice, and squabble' among Frenchmen. What is more, these people, although labelled as 'savages', could teach French atheists sobering lessons concerning the reality of an unseen world.

Years later, having returned to France and witnessed the horrors of the wars of religion, personally surviving the terrible siege of the city of Sancerre, Léry confessed that his brief stay among a primal people in the forests of South America had destroyed the neat categorizations by which people were identified as civilized and uncivilized. He was no longer sure where the 'savages' were to be found and described his regret at not being with the Tupi, 'in whom . . . I have known more frankness than in many over here, who, for their condemnation, bear the title "Christian"'. Here then is a Protestant 'voice of compassion' which, like the Catholic voices we have heard earlier, identified closely and sympathetically with a despised, misrepresented and alas, soon to be destroyed, people, and who, as a result, was compelled to re-read the Bible and to recognize the inadequacies of a received theology.[13]

---

13. I have written concerning Léry and his mission in 'The Forgotten "Grandfather" of Protestant Mission: Perspectives on Globalization from Jean de Léry', *Missiology* XXXIV / 3, July 2006, pp. 349–359.

Reading the Bible in the age of globalization

The conclusion we are compelled to draw from the examples discussed above is that both Catholic and Protestant Christians interpreted the Bible in widely divergent ways at the dawn of the modern world. Some defended the use of violence in mission, while others completely repudiated it; biblical eschatology was used to sanctify imperial ambitions and the spread of 'civilization', while Scripture was also re-read in the light of experience, and new questions, never previously discussed in European theology, were brought to the text. The encounter with new worlds could result therefore, both in an increase in ethnocentrism, as the affirmation of the superiority of one's own culture became stronger than ever, and in the emergence of a critical understanding of the European tradition and a recognition of its distance from the values of the Bible, notwithstanding its claims to be 'Christian'.

It is not possible here to trace the connections between the discovery of the Americas at the end of the fifteenth century and the fully globalized world which emerged five hundred years later following the collapse of the bi-polar situation in which a capitalist West had faced a communist East for most of the twentieth century. Our primary concern is with the fact that while this world-historical development is often publicly celebrated as an inevitable and irreversible phenomenon which will, in the fullness of time, bring freedom, justice and prosperity to the whole earth, it currently creates millions of victims whose cries (like those of the native populations of the New World) often go unheard among the beneficiaries of the system. The sociologist Zygmunt Bauman has concluded that what appears as globalization for some people, resulting in greater freedom, prosperity and mobility, descends uninvited upon others as a 'cruel fate'. In a memorable categorization he suggests that the world's population is increasingly divided between 'tourists' and 'vagabonds'. He writes:

> For the inhabitants of the first world – the increasingly cosmopolitan, extraterritorial world of global businessmen, global culture managers or global academics, state borders are levelled down, as they are dismantled for the world's commodities, capital and finances. For the inhabitants of the second world, the walls built of immigration controls, of residence laws and 'clean streets' and 'zero tolerance' policies, grow taller; the moats separating them from the sites of their desire and of dreamed-of-redemption grow deeper, while all bridges, at the first attempt to cross them, prove to be drawbridges.[14]

Bauman's penetrating and disturbing analysis of the human consequences of globalization serves to underline again the crucial significance of biblical hermeneutics in relation to the practice of mission in our world today. Will the Bible become an increasingly marginalized narrative, treasured by individuals who will find personal peace and comfort in the text, while irrelevant and increasingly forgotten by those who hold the levers of power? Or, more worryingly, might the reverse happen, as a selective reading of the biblical story comes to be deployed by the beneficiaries of globalization in support of this process as it presently exists, so providing a religious justification for the privileges they enjoy? After all, we have seen how Western Christianity and its mission have often been harnessed to the progress of North-Atlantic civilizations, so it is possible to envisage readings of the Bible in

---

14. Zygmunt Bauman, *Globalization: The Human Consequences* (Cambridge: Polity Press, 1998), p. 89.

which globalization becomes a 'sign of the kingdom of God'. Or again, will the Bible be read from the perspective of the victims of global economic and political processes, producing twenty-first-century 'voices of compassion' from a World Christianity compelled to bring a critical, prophetic analysis to bear on the world we now inhabit?

In reflecting on what a biblically-informed response to globalization might look like, I suggest we begin by considering the broad context within which the story of Israel and the church unfolds. Walter Brueggemann has observed that the biblical narratives are set 'always in the shadow of empire'. The imperial powers of Egypt, Assyria, Babylon and Persia weave in and out of the narrative and successively provided the setting within which the covenant people's faith was developed, confessed and deeply challenged. These empires made absolute claims and endeavoured to assimilate conquered peoples within their own dominant cultural and economic systems. While Israel's experience varied under different imperial powers, in every case the Bible bears witness to the nation's struggle to 'maintain its distinct identity and to protect space for its liberated imagination and, consequently, for its distinct covenantal ethic'.[15] It is even more significant for us that this insight can be extended into the New Testament, since the ministry of Jesus and the story of the earliest Christian communities took place beneath the shadow of the greatest empire of all, that of Rome. From the nativity narratives of the Gospels, which so clearly locate the birth of Jesus in the reign of Caesar Augustus and the Roman collaborators in Palestine in the shape of the Herodian dynasty, to the apoca-

---

15. Walter Brueggemann, *Texts That Linger, Words That Explode – Listening to Prophetic Voices* (Minneapolis: Fortress Press, 2000), p. 74.

lypse of John, received on the island of Patmos, the shadow of empire extends across the entire period, constituting a fundamental aspect of the context within which the confession that 'Jesus is Saviour and Lord' was made. Within that setting this core belief was unavoidably controversial, potentially treasonable, and therefore dangerous.

The relevance of this to our concerns with globalization is surely obvious: while the use of the term 'global' to describe the empires of the ancient world would be an anachronism, they *were* characterized by the ambition to dominate the known world and to incorporate all the nations within their spheres of political control and religious belief. In the Old Testament the threat which the empires posed to the covenant faith reached its climax with the Babylonian exile when, 'displaced from their homeland and all its sustaining institutional markers, the power of the Babylonian culture to assimilate and the capacity of the Babylonian economy to substitute satiation for a faith identity' constituted a tremendous threat.[16] But it is in the New Testament that faith confronts this challenge at its greatest extent in the context of an empire which claimed both universality and a sacred destiny as the agent through which human history would reach its ultimate fulfilment. The Roman imperial cult has been described as 'a tool for the affirmation of the world-wide reach of Roman power', and buildings, monuments and altars promoted that cult, embedding 'Roman ideas into the fabric of an eastern city and its public life'.[17]

The response of Israel's sages and prophets (although not always of her kings) to the threat posed by the empires was

---

16. Ibid., p. 82.

17. Davina Lopez, *Apostle to the Conquered: Re-imagining Paul's Mission* (Minneapolis: Fortress Press, 2008), p. 96.

one of *resistance, critique and the warning of judgment.* The power and glory of the empires was not to be denied, but prophecy discerned what lay beneath propaganda and uncovered both the deceptive imperial mythologies which screened out uncomfortable aspects of reality, and an idolatry which exalted human beings to the place which belongs to God alone. The many prophecies of Isaiah, Jeremiah and Ezekiel directed to the nations, which may strike us as negative in tone, were not expressions of racial pride or ethnocentrism, but arose from the perception that the idolatry which under-pinned these powers was accompanied by injustice, violence and death, and stood in direct opposition to the purposes which Israel's liberating God had for the world. Nor is this theme limited to the Old Testament; indeed, it is difficult to imagine a more sobering and terrifying text in relation to globalization than the description of the total collapse and destruction of Babylon (a code-word for imperial Rome) in Revelation 18.

This note of judgment on unjust and brutal politics cannot be ignored today and must have a central place in a response to globalization which is faithful to the Bible. We have heard how the 'voices of compassion' in the fifteenth and sixteenth centuries were those of people who had read the Bible from the underside of European expansionism and felt compelled to warn their compatriots that only deep repentance could turn away the wrath and judgment of a just and holy God. Walter Brueggemann, in an important reflection on the role of the Bible in the contemporary church, suggests that the first task of Christians today is to allow the narrative of Scripture to 'de-script' the powerful story which presently shapes our societies. This process of 'de-scripting', or deconstructing, the dominant worldview is the essential precondition to the task of *'the steady, patient, intentional articulation of an alternative script that we testify will indeed make us safe and joyous'.*[18]

So far in this discussion we have assumed that globalization in the form we know it will be the context within which witness to the truth of the Bible and the God of kindness will continue to be made in the century ahead. But we must also consider the possibility that a world organized for the benefit of the rich and powerful, and in which the suffering of millions of people (many of whom confess Christ as Lord) results in cries of distress which reach into heaven, *is a world on the edge of collapse*. The question therefore cannot be simply, 'How to respond to globalization?' but, how might the Bible be read in a situation in which the present socio-political and economic order implodes? What if the economic crash in the first decade of this century were to be only the overture for a far more spectacular collapse of the whole system? And what if this were then to result in a situation in which new forms of fascism appeared, claiming to be the agents of order and the means of salvation for the global economy? Might it even be that the new rulers of the world would claim that their mission included the re-establishment of 'Christian values' and the defence of a Christian civilization? What biblical themes might then be important for the church's witness in a context in which the idols of our times, despite having been exposed as lifeless and demonic substitutes for the worship of the true Lord of history, were, like the Philistine Dagon, stood back on their feet and accorded ever more frantic devotion?

So much for the theme of *resistance, critique and the warning of judgment*. We need now to consider the fact that the biblical

---

18. Walter Brueggemann, *Mandate to Difference: An Invitation to the Contemporary Church* (Louisville: Westminster John Knox Press, 2007), p. 195, emphasis original.

critique of the abuse of power on the part of the empires of the ancient world is the outcome of the writers' knowledge of *a different script in which real freedom and justice is promised to all nations as they come to worship the God who has shown his salvation to Abraham and his descendants.* In other words, the destiny of the nations is not that which the empires declare it to be, but rather is to discover justice, freedom and community through the worship and love of the God who from the dawn of history has promised his *shalom* to the world.

One of the benefits of recent studies in hermeneutics is the realization that the Bible contains a 'big story'. In Kevin Vanhoozer's words, it is not 'a rag-bag collection of teachings', but 'an integrated drama concerning the unfolding covenant of grace'.[19] That drama commences from the first pages of the Bible and includes overlooked texts which may be about to take on particular significance in relation to the challenge posed by globalization. For example, the 'Table of Nations' in Genesis 10 charts the spread of peoples, each with their own language, and identifies urban locations which were later to be subjected to prophetic critique. This text has no known parallel in the ancient world and serves to affirm the theological fact that the entire world, with its diversity of peoples and their cities, is the object of God's mercy. When, two chapters later, Abram is promised that 'all peoples on earth' will be blessed through his faith, the extent of that blessing has already been mapped out in the Table of Nations. Claus Westermann describes this text as 'the most forceful and heavily underscored statement of the Bible about God's blessing, which extends over the whole earth and the whole

---

19. Kevin Vanhoozer, in John G. Stackhouse (ed.), *Evangelical Futures: A Conversation on Theological Method* (Grand Rapids: Baker Books and Leicester: Apollos, 2000), p. 76.

of human history'.[20] This ecumenical vision pervades the Old Testament to a degree often overlooked; it can be traced in the historical books, is clearly present in the prayers of the psalmists, and surfaces in prophetic statements concerning the nations. After the Babylonian exile the tradition bursts out afresh in the shape of visions which anticipate the display of God's glory 'among the nations', and even to 'the distant islands' (Isa. 66:19).[21]

The same language is found on the lips of the risen Christ, except that now it forms the mandate for the mission of his followers who are told to 'go and make disciples of *all nations*' (Matt. 28:18). The promise implicit in Genesis 10, and explicit in the call of Abram, here reaches its fulfilment; the turning point of the ages has come and the announcement of salvation, of God's great *shalom*, must be made to the entire world. Indeed, this is precisely what happens at Pentecost when 'the wonders of God' are announced in the presence of people 'from every nation of the world'. At the close of the New Testament we hear the echo of Genesis 10 for the final time as the author, confined in a Roman penal colony, catches sight of a transformed world in which a numberless multitude 'from every tribe and language and people and nation' have renounced the idols of empire and come to worship the slain and risen Lamb who alone is worthy to 'receive power and wealth and wisdom and strength' (Rev. 5:9, 12).

---

20. Claus Westermann, *Genesis 1–11 – A Commentary* (Minneapolis: Augsburg Publishing, 1984), pp. 528–530.
21. See James Scott, *Paul and the Nations: The Old Testament and the Jewish Background of Paul's Mission to the Gentiles. With Special Reference to the Destination of Galatians* (Tübingen: JCM Mohr [Paul Siebeck], 1995).

Keeping to the script

What becomes clear from this brief outline of biblical themes is that Scripture contains the resources both to critique the existing form taken by globalization and to develop *an alternative vision of the future of the one world, and the one humankind, created by God*. However, it is far from easy for Christians who benefit from the existing process of globalization to recognize, embrace and act in accordance with this alternative vision. From the very beginning of the biblical narrative, nominal adherence to the demanding, counter-cultural script revealed through the Law and the Prophets was, sooner or later, combined with a way of life shaped by ideas and values utterly alien to it. Almost imperceptibly, ancient Israel sought to combine allegiance to Yahweh with the 'practical politics' of kingship, modelled on the 'way of the world'. A similar process of syncretism, although far too subtle and heavily disguised to be recognized as such by those trapped in compromise, is clearly and repeatedly evident within the New Testament. As the fires of Pentecost die down we again hear prophetic warnings to those whose faith is morphing into little more than a set of intellectual ideas devoid of the power to resist the dominant script of imperial idolatry and materialism. The tendency toward forms of dualism which separate 'faith' from practice, so allowing daily life in the 'real world' to be sealed off from the demands of a covenantal ethic, or from the imperatives of genuine discipleship, are clearly present among the first Christians, provoking a prophetic insistence that true religion is a dynamic, transformative force which creates communities of care and compassion, and enables resistance to the 'pollution of the world' (Jas 1:27). If it was thus *then*, we can hardly be surprised that it should be so *now* when the script of globalization has become universal and is communicated through the most powerful forms of propaganda ever invented. As a result, nominal adherence to the biblical tradition, as classically seen among the churches of Asia Minor described in the early chapters of the book of Revelation, is accompanied by a desperate spiritual lukewarmness, and creates reluctance to face suffering and loss on account of the confession that Jesus, not Caesar – not the free market – is Lord.

Commenting on the situation in North America, Walter Brueggemann says that, although Scripture offers us 'an alternative world' shaped by God's surprising and wonderful newness, the processes of socialization in Western societies have created an ambivalence toward the 'strange world' of the Bible which 'touches every church member, liberal or conservative, and engrosses every minister of whatever ilk'. As a result, Christians in the rich and powerful nations 'are characteristically double-minded, standing between two scripts the way Elijah found Israel standing between Baal and YHWH'.[22]

How might Christians throughout our one world overcome the drift to a Laodicean compromise in which the pursuit of material wealth, and the self-sufficiency which accompanies it, results in blindness to the reality of spiritual bankruptcy? How can World Christianity recover the alternative vision offered to us in the biblical narratives, and then, under the immense pressure of the forces which currently dominate our world, *keep to that script, offering it as good news, and modelling human community shaped by it, to a human family trapped in a worldview that leads to death*? Can Christians in the twenty-first century, like those we have discussed above in the sixteenth century, hear 'another Voice' above the incessant

---

22. Brueggemann, *Mandate to Difference*, p. 201.

din of the modern, electronically connected Babel, as they practice *fellowship* with the poor, the oppressed and the despairing? Can they also hear that 'other Voice' in the cries of the earth itself, as creation groans under the burden of human greed, folly and sin? Can we find examples in the modern, industrialized world of people who have read the Bible from below, and have 'kept to the script' in a way that has brought transformation and hope?

In 1856, with the industrial revolution reaching its peak in Britain, a child was born to a poverty-stricken family in the mining village of Legbrannock in the West of Scotland. The baby was given the names James Keir Hardie, and was to grow up in a home in which illness, debt and suffering were ever-present realities. By the time the boy was old enough to work he was sent to seek the employment which was to be the sole lifeline for a home in which death and sickness left his parents destitute and their cottage without furniture. The young Keir Hardie found a job with a baker whom he described as 'a leading light in the religious life of the city [of Glasgow]'. One morning Hardie, having been nursing his dying brother and supporting a heart-broken mother, arrived at the bakery a few moments late for work and was ordered upstairs to see his Christian employer. He describes the scene:

> I was kept waiting outside the door of the dining room while he said grace – he was noted for his religious zeal – and, on being admitted, found the master and his family seated around a large table . . . I had never before seen such a beautiful room, nor such a table, loaded as it was with food and beautiful things.[23]

23. A. Fenner Brockway, 'James Keir Hardie (1856–1915)', in Hugh Martin (ed.), *Christian Social Reformers of the Nineteenth Century*

The baker humiliated the young man with a lecture on the 'sin of sloth' and warned him that any recurrence of his late arrival would result in instant dismissal. Two days later the boy, his brother's condition worsening, was again moments late at the bakery and the threat of dismissal was carried out, with two week's wages withheld as a punishment. Hardie was overwhelmed by the harshness and injustice of his employer and in his utter despair contemplated suicide. In the event, the experience gave birth to a burning passion for social justice, a deep loathing of religious hypocrisy, and a spiritual quest for an 'alternative script' to the one which shaped the life of his heartless employer. Keir Hardie read and re-read the same Bible which his employer professed to obey, but heard 'another Voice', one which was to lead him into an extraordinary life of service for the poor, and prophetic criticism of a society which formally honoured God, but in reality worshipped at the altars of Mammon.

Later in life, having engaged in militant action to secure basic rights for working people, founded the Independent Labour Party, and entered parliament to campaign for justice and peace, Keir Hardie repeatedly found himself challenging Christians who, he believed, had lost the plot so far as the biblical narrative was concerned, having allowed personal self-interest to take precedence over the example and teaching of Jesus. Perhaps the most dramatic and disturbing incident of this kind is seen in the account of Hardie's intervention

(London: SCM Press, 1933), p. 229. The major, critical biography is Kenneth Morgan, *Keir Hardie: Radical and Socialist* (London: Phoenix Books, 1997). Morgan describes Hardie as 'the supreme prophet' who 'communicated with the industrial masses directly, emotionally, as a working man whose life since childhood had been scarred by conflict and tragedy', p. 289.

to a debate at the annual meetings of the Congregational Churches in Bradford in 1892. It was reported to this assembly of nonconformist ministers that an MP (it was Hardie himself) had said during a debate in the Westminster Parliament, that 'Christianity was dead' and he was glad of this! The speaker deplored this language and said that, while the church should 'see that the surroundings of the poor should be decent', the lower classes should be made to work for a living, and the authorities 'should whip with a cat-o-nine-tails every vagabond who would not work'. As the cheers of the audience died down, Keir Hardie rose and asked permission to speak:

> Mr Keir Hardie, M.P., who was present was . . . allowed to go to the platform to make an explanation . . . What he had said was that the Christianity of the schools was dead, and that the Christianity of Christ was coming to the front. What he desired was a peaceable and gradual settlement of the labour question . . . The reason the Labour Party had turned its back upon the Church was because the Church had turned its back on them ['No, No']. They got respectable congregations on Sunday and preached to please respectability [Cries of 'No, no']. But they did [loud cries of 'No, no' and 'It is false']. They forgot the writhing and suffering mass of humanity outside the walls of their churches [Voices, 'No, no']. . . . In the slums of the cities, men, women and children made in the image of God were being driven down into hell for all eternity, and they had no helping hand stretched out for them [Cries of 'It is false' and interruption]. It was a disgrace to the Christian ministers of England [Loud cries of dissent].[24]

---

24. 'The Congregational Union at Bradford', *The British Weekly*, 13 October 1892, p. 401.

Keir Hardie MP

Hardie's speech was drowned out by the heckling from the assembly and, while the chairman appealed for a fair hearing, 'amid some confusion Mr. Keir Hardie left the platform'.

As with the opponents of the *conquistadores*, Keir Hardie's voice was one of compassion, coming from below, from the underside of a sharply divided society. He not only demanded justice for the poor, but supported the liberation of women and was a courageous and uncompromising opponent of militarism and war. He challenged both the monarchy and aristocratic privileges and was a vocal opponent of British imperialism. The First World War was a terrible blow to him and he was heartbroken that working people across Europe ignored his call not to engage in military action against each other. Above all, he revered the life and teaching of Jesus and near the end of his life said that if he were to live again he would devote himself 'to the advocacy of the Gospel of Christ'.[25]

In the twenty-first century new 'voices of compassion' are being raised from the underside of the globalization process, and it seems certain that their numbers will grow. The critical question is whether they will be heard by Christians who benefit from the existing world system, especially when they reveal the extent to which rich believers are trapped in the ambivalence toward the biblical story which we have described in this chapter. Our hope and prayer must be that the followers of Christ in both North and South may indeed hear each other, and in doing so will learn how to listen *together* to that 'other Voice' which addresses us through the Law and the Prophets, and supremely by the 'Word made flesh' who dwells among us. It is precisely this hope which has led theologians from across a range of traditions to propose that globalization presents us with an opportunity to recover the *catholicity* of the Church of Christ. Seen in this light, globalization is less a threat to faith and more an opportunity to display within history a foretaste of the new humankind made possible by the redemption provided by Christ. As Max Stackhouse has said, 'Globalization involves the possibility of a gracious recovery and recasting of the catholicity of the faith'.[26] The

---

25. Fenner Brockway, 'James Keir Hardie', p. 239.

26. Max Stackhouse, quoted in Donald Lewis, 'Globalization: The Problem of Definition and Future Areas of Historical Enquiry', in Mark Hutchinson and Ogbu Kalu (eds.), *A Global Faith: Essays on Evangelicalism and Globalization* (Sydney: Centre for the Study of Australian Christianity, 1998), p. 39. Stackhouse has edited an important series of volumes under the overall title, *God and Globalization: Theological Ethics and the Spheres of Life*, published

pathway to such a goal may be long and difficult, but both the new 'voices of compassion' emerging from the Global South and believers from the old heartlands in the North, may join together in re-reading the biblical texts and discovering afresh what it will mean at this specific point in history to be the ambassadors of the new age in the midst of the old.[27]

At the conclusion of a book bearing the provocative title, *Is The Reformation Over?*, Mark Noll and Carolyn Nystrom, having undertaken an intensive study of post-Vatican II developments within Roman Catholicism, conclude that the question in their title is not really the right one to be asking:

> It may be more to the point to ask other questions: Is God truly going to draw people from every tribe and tongue and people and nation – and major Christian traditions – to worship together the Lamb who was slain? Can he really make of them – all these tongues and people and traditions – a single kingdom united in the body of his Son Jesus Christ? Should believers in the all-powerful, all-merciful God doubt that such signs and wonders might still take place?[28]

---

by Trinity Press International. See too the important work by the Roman Catholic theologian Robert Schreiter, *The New Catholicity: Theology Between the Global and the Local* (New York: Orbis Books, 2004).

27. The phrase comes from Kevin Vanhoozer, '"One Rule to Rule Them All?" Theological Method in an Era of World Christianity', in Craig Ott and Harold Netland (eds.), *Globalizaing Theology: Belief and Practice in an Era of World Christianity* (Grand Rapids: Baker Academic and Nottingham: Apollos, 2007), p. 125.

28. Mark Noll and Carolyn Nystrom, *Is The Reformation Over? An Evangelical Assessment of Contemporary Roman Catholicism* (Grand Rapids: Baker Academic, 2005), p. 251.

The letter to the Romans and mission in a troubled, urban world

A crucial feature of the troubled world we have described in these studies is that the process of modernization has been accompanied by the massive growth of cities. To an extent that is entirely without precedent, this is an *urbanizing* world. During the past decade much of my work has involved the study of this aspect of our contemporary situation, and this has meant both research into the historical and sociological dimensions of this process and a re-reading of the Bible with particular attention given to the urban context of Scripture itself.[1] This has led to many surprises, one of which concerns our understanding of Paul's greatest letter.

Written at some point between AD 55 and 64, this letter was addressed to 'all in Rome who are loved by God and called to be his holy people' (1:7). It is, therefore, self-evidently directed to

---

1. The result of these studies can be seen in my book, *Seeking a City With Foundations: Theology for an Urban World* (Nottingham: IVP, 2011). The discussion of Romans in that book (pp. 197–205) is here enlarged and extended.

the disciples of Jesus living in the greatest city the world had then seen. Despite never having been in Rome, Paul was well informed concerning the physical and socio-economic conditions in which his hearers lived their lives and was aware of the enormous challenges presented to their faith in Christ by the all-pervasive ideology of the empire of which Rome was the centre. This being so, the opening greeting is enough on its own to indicate the absurdity of context-less readings of the letter to the Romans and it suggests that any interpretation which ignores the actual situation of its first recipients is bound to mislead us with regard to the apostle's message and purpose. And yet, throughout the history of biblical interpretation, Romans has repeatedly been discussed in commentaries and studies which have taken little or no cognizance of the actual situation of first urban Christians in this vast, deeply divided city.

The interpretation of Paul's letter to the Romans in Christian history

The letter of Paul to the Romans has played a major part in shaping the theology and practice of Christianity across the centuries, especially within the Western tradition. Augustine of Hippo (354–430) describes how hearing someone read aloud from this letter was the trigger for his own conversion to Christianity, and his subsequent work drew heavily upon this text. Augustine's influence on Western Christianity, both Catholic and Protestant, was immense, and can be seen clearly in yet another key historical figure, Martin Luther. His anguished search for a gracious God led him to Paul, and in 1515 he found Augustine confirming his own reading of the letter to the Romans, resulting in the Reformation doctrine of justification by faith and the rejection of medieval perversions of Paul's gospel. It has been said that 'through Augustine

Romans has continued to influence western thought about the human subject down to Marx, Freud, existentialism, and phenomenology'.[2]

In the early twentieth century, Romans was yet again the catalyst for a spiritual revolution, this one associated with the name of the great Swiss theologian, Karl Barth. Barth's famous commentary on Romans was first published in 1919 and fourteen years later, when the English translation appeared, he recalled: 'When I first wrote it . . . it required only a little imagination for me to hear the sounds of the guns booming away in the north.'[3] In the shadow of the carnage of the First World War the young pastor realized the bankruptcy of the liberal tradition and, rediscovering Paul's letter, broke his ties with European culture-Protestantism. Barth wrote that he knew what it was like year after year to mount the steps of the pulpit conscious of the responsibility to understand and interpret the Bible, 'yet utterly incapable' of doing so because his education had left him in a position in which 'all hope of engaging in the dignity of understanding and interpretation [had] been surrendered'.[4] The opening comments of Barth's commentary on Romans already sound the notes which were to become central themes in his theology: 'The Gospel is not a religious message to inform mankind of their divinity or to tell them how they may become divine. The Gospel proclaims a God utterly distinct from men.'[5]

---

2. R. Morgan, 'Romans', in Adrian Hastings (ed.), *The Oxford Companion to Christian Thought* (Oxford: Oxford University Press, 2000), pp. 626–627.

3. Karl Barth, *The Epistle to the Romans*, 'Preface to the English Edition' (London: Oxford University Press, 1968), p. v.

4. Ibid., p. 9.

5. Ibid., p. 28.

Paradigm change in Pauline studies

In the 1970s questions began to be asked concerning the tradition of Pauline interpretation which had begun with Augustine, in which Romans was understood as stressing Christianity's radical break with what was believed to be Jewish legalism, and the gospel was interpreted as primarily a message concerning God's justification of individual sinners. The Lutheran scholar Krister Stendahl expressed growing doubts concerning this received tradition with startling clarity: 'It will be my contention . . . that the main lines of Pauline interpretation . . . have for many centuries been out of touch with one of the most basic questions and concerns that shaped Paul's thinking in the first place: the relation between Jews and Gentiles.'[6] Stendahl's reading of Paul, like that of Barth before him, had a particular historical context, but whereas the latter was shaped by the First World War and the collapse of Western civilization, Stendahl's new reading of Paul came in the aftermath of the Second World War and, in particular, the Holocaust. Augustine, who Stendahl describes as 'the first truly Western man', is seen as responsible for a shift toward a focus on the individual soul which eventually resulted in a culture in which, as Stendahl puts it, 'Man turned in on himself, infatuated and absorbed by the question, not of when God will send deliverance in the history of salvation, but how God is working in the individual soul'.[7]

Stendahl describes the introspective conscience as 'a Western development and a Western plague' which, 'having entered the theological bloodstream' of Europe, came to

---

6. Krister Stendahl, *Paul among Jews and Gentiles and Other Essays* (Philadelphia: Fortress Press, 1976), p. 1.

7. Ibid., p. 17.

dominate the culture during and after the Reformation. With the coming of modernity this tradition took a secular form in the work of Sigmund Freud. Yet, while this concern for the interior life of the individual was claimed to be derived from the New Testament, Stendahl emphatically declares, 'Paul himself was never involved in this pursuit'. Describing the articulation of the gospel which dominated the churches of the Western world at the time at which he wrote, Stendahl said that it left the impression that the message of the New Testament is 'a little private matter of individual ethics' which scarcely relates to 'the greater issues which people really have on their minds'. The twentieth century, like the era in which Romans was written, was a period characterized by fear and a sense of being at the mercy of forces which were perceived to be both powerful and mysterious. Paul's writings, and especially Romans, can speak afresh into such a context only, Stendahl insists, 'if we restore Paul to his fullness and do not translate him into a biblical proof-text for Reformation doctrines'.[8]

The work of scholars like Krister Stendahl can be described as the beginning of a paradigm shift in Pauline studies. As is clear from the quotations above, the fresh perspectives emerging from such scholarship involved the claim that Paul had been misread within the Western tradition as the consequence of the distorting effect of a set of cultural lenses which forced him to answer different questions than those which really concerned him in the first century. This radical claim has of course been controversial and, as with paradigm shifts generally, has been vigorously resisted by those who defend the received tradition. It is not my task here to discuss these issues, even less to attempt to reach conclusions concerning a continuing debate

8. Ibid., pp. 39–40.

which is complex and touches on matters about which there are deep sensitivities. However, the importance of the concerns raised by those who argue that we must listen afresh to Paul within his first-century context can be illustrated with reference to Barth's famous commentary. The first sentence of this 1919 book reads thus: 'Paul, as a child of his age, addressed his contemporaries.' However, this statement, which clearly indicates Barth's awareness of the importance of paying attention to the horizon of the biblical world, is immediately undermined by the words which follow: 'It is, however, far more important that, as Prophet and Apostle of the Kingdom of God, he veritably speaks to all men of every age.' Then, as though to make quite clear the relative *insignificance* of the original context to a proper understanding of Paul's message, Barth adds, 'The differences between then and now . . . are, in fact, purely trivial'.[9]

Karl Barth's scepticism concerning historical criticism is understandable when we recall his own context, in which an arid, academic scholarship rendered the pulpit powerless to

---

9. Barth, *Romans*, p. 1. Three years later in the preface to the second edition, Barth responded to the furore created by his commentary and uses language which sounds a rather different note: 'There is no difference of opinion with regard to the need of applying historical criticism as a prolegomenon to the understanding of the Epistle. So long as the critic is occupied in this preliminary work I follow him carefully and gratefully.' Barth cites Luther and Calvin as examples of 'genuine understanding and interpretation' and says of the latter, ' . . . how energetically Calvin, having first established what stands in the text, sets himself to rethink the whole material and to wrestle with it, till the walls which separate the sixteenth century from the first become transparent!', ibid., p. 7.

challenge a dominant culture which acknowledged religion only in as far as it provided an ideological underpinning for the Western expansionist project. Indeed, Barth's work was itself prophetic and liberating, as Robert Jewett recognizes in the preface to his own recent commentary on Romans. Jewett describes how he wrestled 'night after sleepless night' with the great Swiss theologian's earlier commentary, and how this book helped him through a spiritual crisis by leading to the realization 'that the gospel challenged my dearest cultural premises'.[10] Nonetheless, Jewett's own mature reflections on Romans take a very different line from Barth in relation to the crucial importance of understanding the original historical-cultural setting of the letter and, in doing so, illustrate the fruits of the 'new perspective' on Paul in relation to the Christian mission today. After lamenting the way in which words and phrases in Romans have been burdened 'with theo-logical content held with absolute certainty by particular churches and groups', Jewett continues:

> The transforming gospel about God's righteousness regaining control of all disobedient persons and institutions by overturning their guises of superior honor is thus domesticated into an ideology favouring one side or another in long-standing theological battles . . . The message of Romans is thus transformed into a new kind of theological law, producing bondage just as inexorably as Paul argues it always does. At the

---

10. Robert Jewett, *Romans – A Commentary*, Hermeneia (Minneapolis: Fortress Press, 2007), p. xv. Citations below to *Romans* are to this major commentary. In an earlier work Jewett outlined his approach to Romans in a brief and accessible outline of its content and significance. See Robert Jewett, *Romans*, Basic Bible Commentary (Nashville: Abingdon Press, 1988).

same time, the distinctive historical and social background of the Roman audience and Paul's rhetorical purpose in addressing them are typically dealt with in the introductions to Romans commentaries but play virtually no role in the interpretative process.[11]

Our concern here is precisely with 'the distinctive historical and social background of the Roman audience' of Paul's letter, since it is the knowledge of this context which provides us with a vital interpretative bridge between then and now. In a collection of essays published in 1994 under the title *Paul the Apostle to America*, Robert Jewett suggested that the cultural lenses which distort our readings of the New Testament are not simply the result of the influence of the *Western* tradition, but, more specifically, of aspects of *European* Christianity. The centuries-long history of religious violence and conflict in Europe, much of it arising from the political nature of rival confessional statements, made it difficult for European Christians to hear Paul's message of reconciliation, healing and hope. As a result European scholars tended to 'downplay the egalitarian joy of early Pauline communities' and 'to discount the evidence of their remarkable solidarity'.[12] Hierarchical structures embedded within European societies throughout the long era of Christendom 'tend to be imposed on the organizational structure of those early communities', so that the radical nature of the Pauline churches is over-looked. In addition, the European mindset is unsympathetic to Paul's apocalyptic hope, with the result that the prevailing

---

11. Jewett, *Romans*, p. 2.
12. Robert Jewett, *Paul the Apostle to America. Cultural Trends and Pauline Scholarship* (Louisville: Westminster/John Knox Press, 1994), p. 8.

pessimism (which many New World observers have detected within Europe) blunts – if it does not actually eliminate – the New Testament's radiant vision of a transformed world. In Jewett's words,

> Paul was a revolutionary who saw a new creation coming. Christ had defeated the principalities and powers, and soon the bridgeheads of hope in the tiny house churches and tenement churches would expand to cover the world, bringing the age of pessimism and cynicism to an end.[13]

New light on ancient Rome

The mention of 'house churches' and 'tenement churches' in this passage brings us to the particular aspect of the context of the ancient world which is of interest to us, namely, the fact that, to a degree which was historically unprecedented, this was *an urban world*. Jewett identifies Wayne Meeks' landmark study, *The First Urban Christians,* as 'the most fundamental departure from the approach shaped by European orthodoxy'. Meeks attempted to write 'a social history of the urbanized groups of Pauline Christians', and in doing so, 'established the revolutionary, apocalyptic, and counter-cultural ethos of these charismatic, converted communities, showing their commitment to egalitarianism in the midst of the hierarchical structures of the culture both inside and outside the church'.[14] Jewett quotes Meeks' description of the first urban Christians as people with 'a kind of double vision',

---

13. Ibid., p. 11.

14. Ibid., p. 25. See Wayne Meeks, *The First Urban Christians. The Social World of the Apostle Paul* (New Haven: Yale University Press, 1983).

seeing on the one hand the phenomenal world around them, with all its injustices and inequality, while at the same time experiencing 'the strange new world of the creating, caring, and judging God, of the crucified Messiah raised from the dead'. Meeks comments that within the meetings of these small groups, 'this other world seems more vivid than the ordinary one' and he suggests that everyone 'who craves a vision of a juster, kinder world' has something to learn from them.[15]

Let us return to the opening address of this letter which ends with the greeting, 'To all in Rome who are loved by God and called to be his holy people . . . ' (1:7). These deceptively simple words are pregnant with meaning in relation to the context of the original recipients of this document. By this time Rome was the greatest city the world had seen, with a population of almost one million people, most of whom were crammed into an area in which population density far exceeded that of any modern city in Europe or America. The glory of classical Rome, which still provides us with the dominant images of this city, obscures the grim reality of overcrowding in appalling conditions which was the lot of the vast majority of the inhabitants of the city. Modern New York, with a population density of forty-one inhabitants per acre, is seen today as a world city with a dense population, whereas in ancient Rome the ratio was 300 people per acre. Put another way, the density of population in ancient Rome was more than twice that of the modern Indian city of Kolkata. This pattern of urban overcrowding was reproduced in cities throughout the Roman Empire, although nowhere else did

15. Quoted by Jewett, *Paul the Apostle to America*, p. 25. The original source is Wayne Meeks, *The Moral World of the First Christians* (Philadelphia: Westminster Press, 1986), pp. 98–120.

population density rival that of the imperial capital. Roman writers such as Juvenal record in graphic detail the practical consequences of such overcrowding in regard to everyday life, describing how, attempting to move along the streets, he was 'blocked by a surging crowd in front, and by a dense mass of people pressing in on us from behind'. To the difficulty of progressing on the ground was added the perils of what might descend from the sky; the same writer reports, 'There's death in every window . . . you can but hope, and put up a piteous prayer in your heart, that they may be content to pour down on you the contents of their slop-basins'. Evidence of this kind suggests that the experience of the city as a place of light, beauty and well-being was given to a very select group of elite people; by contrast, for the vast majority of Rome's inhabitants daily life was lived in 'narrow streets packed with pedestrians and merchants, winding alleys where one dodged rubbish flung from the windows above, and rows of tenement slums bursting with occupants'.[16]

Given this urban context the question that begs a response concerns the recipients of Paul's letter; who were the inhabitants of Rome who are said to be 'loved by God and called to be saints'? It has often been claimed that the earliest Christian communities in the city met in 'house churches' with the permission and support of wealthy patrons who were sympathetic to the new faith. Jewett detects in this widely held assumption another example of the negative influence of

---

16. Moyer Hubbard, *Christianity in the Greco-Roman World: A Narrative Introduction* (Peabody: Hendrickson Publishers, 2010), p. 142. This is an excellent survey of the context of Christianity in the ancient world; in particular the section on 'City and Society' on pp. 111–167 provides much valuable material on the urban setting of Pauline Christianity.

European culture on exegesis in that the communal language which pervades Paul's writing suggests radical forms of community among people at the lowest levels of society. This language has been reinterpreted in a manner which makes it fit neatly with 'the polite circumstances of modern churches where members live in private homes and gather infrequently for worship in church buildings'.[17] Studies of Paul's language, and especially of the list of people named at the end of the letter to the Romans (16:1–16), point to the conclusion that the bulk of the members of these primitive Christian communities were slaves, or former slaves, so that the 'saints' addressed by Paul were overwhelmingly people of low status, struggling to exist close to, or below, the level of economic subsistence. The most likely area of ancient Rome in which such people would have lived has been identified as specific districts known to have been inhabited by immigrants, where conditions were appalling and high-rise slum dwellings proliferated.[18] The 'saints' who are addressed in this letter, and *for whom it is, in its entirety, written,* are primarily people at the bottom end of the pyramidal social structure of Roman society, living 'in dangerously high and overcrowded *insulae*', or tenement blocks. Philip Esler provides a dramatic description of the Roman slums:

---

17. Jewett, *Paul the Apostle to America*, p. 74.

18. Jewett cites the research of Peter Lampe who 'identifies the precise districts in the city where Christianity got its start'. In both places described by Lampe, Trastavere and Porta Campena, meetings in 'house churches' would have been impossible since these districts contained 'the most densely populated section of the city with the highest proportion of high-rise slum dwellings' in Rome, Jewett, *Paul the Apostle to America*, p. 78.

Because of Rome's huge population, settled on a comparatively small area, there was always a shortage of land for housing it. While the elite lived in their atrium-style *domus*, the rest of the population generally made do by renting apartments in the numerous tenement blocks . . . Construction techniques were poor, with foundations too shallow and walls too thin, and, not surprisingly, the tenements often collapsed and were exposed to great risk from fire. The inhabitants of the upper floors had less chance of escape if fire took hold.[19]

Paul's gospel in the imperial city

It is not difficult to imagine the profound significance of a message directed to slum dwelling immigrants in the context we have described, assuring them that they are *loved by God*. The love of God becomes a central theme in this letter; it is said to be *'poured out'* into the hearts of believers (5:5), and to be the absolute guarantee of both their human dignity and of the conquest of the hostile, degrading and dehumanizing powers which confronted them at almost every moment of their existence in the Roman slums (8:35–39). The experience of this impartial and overwhelming love of God provides the

---

19. Philip Esler, *Conflict and Identity in Romans: The Social Setting of Paul's Letter* (Minneapolis: Fortress Press, 2003), pp. 82–83. Some scholars have argued that the early Christian movement was entirely located among the poor. Justin Meggitt describes Paul's own social and economic situation as that of 'the arduous and bitter experience of the urban poor', and he claims that the first followers of Jesus in the cities of the Empire *'en masse* shared the bleak material existence which was the lot of 99% of the inhabitants of the Empire'. *Paul, Poverty and Survival* (Edinburgh: T&T Clark, 1998), pp. 96–99.

resources and dynamic for the transformation of inter-personal relationships, shattering 'the pattern of this world' and creating revolutionary communities of mutual love (12:2, 9; 13:8–10). The radical nature of this message can be appreci-ated only when the socio-cultural context of the ancient world, especially in the form of the system of honour and shame which structured all human relationships, is properly understood. Roman society was both hierarchical and patri-archal in the extreme, with conflicting relationships at every level between rich and poor, male and female, slave and free, Roman and 'barbarian'. At the apex of the social pyramid, the imperial family and those supporting them, representing a minute proportion of the population, possessed staggering wealth, while below them a small segment made up of merchants, military veterans and others able to acquire a small surplus, existed with some degree of security. However, for the vast majority of people in Rome and throughout the Empire (many estimates put the figure at or near 90% of the population) life was lived at or below subsistence level, continually on the edge of survival. Moyer Hubbard sums up the situation as follows, 'The grim reality of life in the first century was abject poverty on a monumental scale. It was not so much a collection of societies consisting of the haves and have-nots *but simply of the have nots*'.[20]

The social structure of Rome was kept in place both by the values of honour and shame, which dictated the nature of all human relationships and served to embed individuals in their allotted place within society, whether high or low, and by the overarching ideological narrative of the empire, according to which Rome was the divinely appointed agent of the

---

20. Hubbard, *Christianity in the Greco-Roman World*, p. 144, emphasis added.

'salvation' of the world. When Octavian defeated Mark Anthony at the battle of Actium in 31 BC and became the undisputed ruler of the empire, receiving the title 'Augustus' four years later, he became the 'master patron' of a populace obliged to give him due honour. The emperor was praised in religious language which confessed him both as 'saviour' and the bringer of peace to a troubled world. The socio-economic pyramid was thus accompanied by what has been called a 'pyramid of honour', enabling a surprisingly small number of officials to rule the empire 'using a combination of force, propaganda, and patronage', held together by '"the workings of honour and pride", which provided "the underpinnings of loyalty and gratitude for benefactions" that made the empire functional'.[21]

The mention of 'force' is a reminder of the violence and brutality which was deployed to sustain this system. The Roman legions conquered and dominated subject nations with great violence. Christopher Kelly describes how the military triumphs of the empire were celebrated in the city of Rome in 'monuments glorifying the advance of Roman rule', by grand victory arches, statues of heroes, and temples 'brilliantly emblazoned with the spoils of war'. As Rome extended its domination by military conquests in both east and west, the city witnessed ever more lavish spectacles in which 'the killing fields of empire were re-enacted in the very heart of the capital'. Cheering crowds praised the victorious legions and rejoiced in the destruction of the enemies of the empire, applauding as thousands of prisoners were put to death. It has been estimated that Julius Caesar's campaigns in Gaul resulted

---

21. Jewett, *Romans*, p. 49. The quotation within this passage is from J. E. Lendon, *Empire of Honour: The Art of Government in the Roman World* (Oxford: Clarendon Press, 1997).

in the death of a million enemy combatants and the enslaving of another million.[22] In addition, the execution by crucifixion of those perceived to present a challenge to imperial power and ideology sent a very public signal to subject peoples concerning the consequences of violations of the laws of honour and submission. And, of course, there was the arena and the games in which men and beasts fought each other to the death in bloody spectacles watched by vast crowds. Alison Futrell has clearly demonstrated the *political* purpose of the Roman arena. The amphitheatres which became key features of the skylines of many imperial cities, were developed in a political context and were designed to 'enhance spectacles used in the furtherance of a political agenda'.

> Human beings were often hunted by animals, as the arena housed the execution of Roman law in the literal execution of those who transgressed the dictates of the state. This was the Roman way of commemorating the triumph of civilization over a bestiality identified, in the arena, with a challenge to the hegemony of Rome.[23]

Consider then, the message of God's unconditional love, a love *experienced* in the heart, addressing 'the hidden wounds of shame' of people at the basement level of this obscenely unjust society, and it becomes dramatically clear why Jesus, the crucified Messiah, gained such a following in the slums of

22. Christopher Kelly, *The Roman Empire. A Very Short Introduction* (Oxford: Oxford University Press, 2006), pp. 13–14.

23. Alison Futrell, *Blood in the Arena. The Spectacle of Roman Power* (Austin: University of Texas Press, 1997), p. 10. See also, Roland Auguet, *Cruelty and Civilization: The Roman Games* (London: Routledge, 1994).

ancient Rome. Paul is careful to point out that the love of God poured into the hearts of the saints, gives birth to a hope which *does not cause shame* (5:5). The dynamics of shame and honour are addressed throughout the letter to the Romans, and in a moving passage Robert Jewett summarizes the apostle's purpose in relation to the endless contest for honour and the boasting of one's superior status which it generated:

> Given the mind-set produced by Greco-Roman and Jewish cultures, [Paul] cannot eliminate boasting altogether; it is bred in the bone so to speak. Nevertheless, he hopes to change its form into a celebration of the glory of God and of the love of Christ that sustains believers through every adversity. The traditional forms of boasting are no longer needed to gain and sustain their honor in the face of a hostile world. Christ's blood that was shed for the undeserving fills that need, and its consoling message is conveyed by the Spirit directly to the vulnerable hearts of believers who thereby are enabled to live in confident hope no matter how badly they are treated. In Christ, adversity has lost its power to shame.[24]

Not ashamed of the gospel

The first chapter of Romans begins with the statement that Paul understands his calling as a servant and an apostle, 'set apart for *the gospel of God*' (1:1). The following verses are peppered with repeated references to the 'gospel' (1:2, 9, 15, 16–17). Few words are more familiar and prominent in Christian circles today and it is widely assumed that the use of this terminology in the practice of contemporary mission and evangelism corresponds to the meaning intended by Paul.

---

24. Jewett, *Romans*, p. 357.

What this would actually mean is that Paul, addressing the followers of Jesus in the imperial city we have described above, knowing the circumstances of their lives as marginal people without hope in a world structured by a political and religious ideology which claimed to be the agent of universal 'salvation', would offer them a message limited to personal salvation and the hope of heaven. It is enough, surely, to state the matter in this way to realize that such a 'gospel' would hardly be heard as 'good news' at all, so that, within its first-century context, this (over)familiar term must have had a different meaning from that which it has come to signify in modern times. Like so much else written by Paul in Romans, this word has a *double* reference, so that it was neither a neutral term, devoid of pre-existing content and meaning, nor could it have been restricted to an enclosed area of life designated as 'religious' or 'spiritual'. Neil Elliot observes that many of Paul's most significant theological phrases, including 'Lord', 'Son of God' and 'gospel', resonated with imperial overtones since they were widely and constantly deployed as the language of imperial propaganda.[25] The 'gospel of God' is thus set over against the 'gospel of the Caesars'; the destiny of the nations is not that announced by Rome – to be absorbed within the empire and forcibly subjected to its rule – but rather, to find true freedom and justice under the reign of Messiah-Jesus. It is this alternative vision which motivates and drives Paul's mission, creating an *obligation* to announce the gospel in, and far

25. Neil Elliot, *The Arrogance of Nations. Reading Romans in the Shadow of Empire* (Minneapolis: Fortress Press, 2008), p. 44. See the same author's 'The Apostle Paul and Empire', in Richard Horsley (ed.), *In the Shadow of Empire: Reclaiming the Bible as a History of Faithful Resistance* (Louisville: Westminster John Knox Press, 2008), pp. 97–116.

beyond, Rome, so that the nations presently subjected to imperial rule might find the freedom and justice which flows from the work of the crucified and risen Jesus. As N. T. Wright has said, Paul's gospel carried 'two sets of resonances', one rooted in the Old Testament, especially the prophetic promises of comfort for Israel and hope for the nations, and the other concerned with the existing context 'where *gospel* would mean the celebration of the accession, or birth, of a king or emperor'. Paul's gospel was thus 'a royal proclamation aimed at challenging other royal proclamations'. He continues,

> The main challenge was to the lordship of Caesar, which, though 'political' from our point of view as well as in the first century, was also profoundly 'religious'. Caesar demanded worship as well as 'secular' obedience: not just taxes, but sacrifices. He was well on his way to becoming the supreme divinity in the Greco-Roman world, maintaining his vast empire not simply by force – although there was of course plenty of that – but by the development of a flourishing religion that seemed to be trumping most others either by absorption or greater attraction. Caesar . . . had provided justice and peace to the whole world. He was therefore to be hailed as Lord and trusted as Savior. *This is the world in which Paul announced that Jesus, the Jewish Messiah, was Savior and Lord.*[26]

---

26. N. T. Wright, 'Paul's Gospel and Caesar's Empire', in Richard Horsley (ed.), *Paul and Politics* (Harrisburg: Trinity Press International, 2000), p. 168, emphasis added. See also Tom Wright's *What Saint Paul Really Said* (Oxford: Lion Publishing, 1997) which, despite its unfortunate title, provides an excellent description of Paul's gospel within the context of the Roman world.

Of course, this means that Paul's gospel was far from being an innocuous religious message which posed no challenge to the dominant worldview. On the contrary, while certainly not advocating insurrection, the message contained in the letter to the Romans exposed the fraudulent claims of the empire again and again, offering a radical vision of an alternative way of being a human family, and of a world in which justice, peace and love become realities. This being the case, it is little wonder that the Christ-followers in Rome should fall under the suspicion of a regime which went to extraordinary lengths to keep new religious sects under control. The fact that believers in Christ lived in the poorest parts of the city, where the most marginalized of people, including despised immigrants, crowded into dangerous tenements, meant that they were automatically suspect. Those in power 'were conscious of the explosive mix of "outsiders", extraneous people who congregated in the *insulae*'.[27] It has even been suggested that the content of the letter to the Romans was the cause of Paul's own arrest and execution, and that when those in power realized the meaning of Paul's gospel, reading it as a direct challenge to the Caesar cult, they charged him with treason against the empire. Dieter Georgi argues that once the Roman authorities understood Paul to be denying the right of Caesar Claudius to claim the heavens as a reward for his saving acts for the world, and to be undermining the boast of Nero that he had ushered in the golden age, replacing these imperial claims with the proclamation that a Jewish peasant crucified in Palestine was worthy to be honoured as Saviour and Lord, he was condemned to death.[28]

---

27. Dieter Georgi, *The City in the Valley: Biblical Interpretation and Urban Theology* (Atlanta: Society for Biblical Literature, 2005), p. 148.

28. Ibid., pp. 158–159.

Reading Romans in a globalized, urban world

How shall we then read the letter to the Romans today in a world in which the majority of Christians are once again poor and oppressed, with millions living in slum conditions in the burgeoning cities of the Global South? This is not an easy question for believers in the privileged and powerful nations of the modern world to answer. Between Paul and the churches of the Western world today there are centuries of historical development during which Christianity ceased being either an *urban* faith, or a *missionary* religion. With the collapse of Rome and the invasion of the barbarian peoples from the north, Christianity in Europe was transformed into a rural and agricultural religion, leaving it largely bereft of the spiritual and theological resources required to meet the challenge of an urban world. As far as mission is concerned, when those same barbarian invaders flooded into the church, reshaping Christianity in various ways, mission became both unnecessary and impossible, with the rare exception of the brave souls who moved beyond the continent-wide sphere controlled by the church and engaged the benighted peoples who lived beyond the reach of Christian civilization.

However, we are now witnesses of a series of interlocking historical developments which, taken together, move us beyond Christendom and usher in a new era in which the New Testament, including the letter to the Romans, can be read with eyes no longer clouded by the presuppositions of the Constantinian legacy. The *collapse* of Christendom, and the resulting crisis for the churches of the West, the massive *growth* of Christianity across the Global South, especially in Pentecostal forms in contexts of urban poverty and suffering, and the accelerating *expansion* of cities, driven by economic and ideological forces which pose similar questions to those we have seen Paul expressing with regard to the Roman imperium, all of these developments in our world presage a new epoch in Christian history. The Hispanic theologian Justo González comments that we are living 'in a time of vast changes in the church's self-understanding', and that the consequences of the shifts taking place today 'will be more drastic than those which took place in the sixteenth century'. The loss of Christendom, González says, should not be lamented since it opens up the possibility that the meaning of Scripture may become clearer to us as truth is seen to consist not in abstract, intellectual concepts, but rather as 'closely bound with bread and wine, with justice and peace, with a coming Reign of God – a Reign not over pure ideas and disembodied souls but over a new society and a renewed history'.[29]

What role will Paul's letter to the Romans play in this tremendous development? The answer, of course, is that we do not know, since we stand at the very beginning of a new era in which the contributions of a global Christian community to our understanding of Scripture are in their infancy. González points out that one of the features of the transformation taking place around us is that whole swathes of the human population, taught to be silent and passive recipients of the ideas and values of their superiors and betters, are today finding their voices. Ethnic minorities, women and children, people who 'for reasons of class, nationality, sex, age, sexual orientation and the like, will no longer be silent'.[30] What this suggests is that the most significant insights into Paul's message are likely to come from *below*, from people whose

---

29. Justo González, *Mañana: Christian Theology from a Hispanic Perspective* (Nashville: Abingdon Press, 1990), p. 50.

30. Ibid., p. 48.

socio-economic situation in a globalized world corresponds closely to that of the majority of the *original recipients of this letter in the slums of the megacity of Rome*. This fact is highlighted by Peter Oakes' use of archaeological evidence in the ruins of Pompeii to construct an imagined 'house church' in first-century Rome. Such a group certainly included slaves, including women who were almost routinely subjected to sexual exploitation. How would such followers of Jesus have heard Paul's letter? If, as was the case, they lacked final control over their own bodies, how might they cope with the tensions which the new faith inevitably set up? A slave girl whose owner expected her to flirt with customers in the bar in which she worked, and whose income derived from such activities kept her and her children alive, brings questions to the text of Romans which are unlikely ever to be heard in the middle-class suburbs in which most Western churches are located today. Oakes concludes that, while there is a place for the academic study of Romans, 'there is also a place for thinking about how it sounds to people at ground level'.[31] Indeed, in the twenty-first century we must do more than *think about this*, we must *ask our brothers and sisters in the slums of Sao Paulo, Nairobi and Mumbai* how they hear this ancient letter and what following Jesus means in practice in their daily lives.

Reading Romans in a troubled world

Let me conclude by identifying just three of the issues which arise from the reading of Paul's greatest letter with careful attention to its original context. *First, what will it mean in*

---

31. Peter Oakes, *Reading Romans in Pompeii: Paul's Letter at Ground Level* (London: SPCK, 2009), p. 179.

the twenty-first century for believers around the world to obey the injunction not to 'conform to the pattern of this world' (12:2)? Paul urges the saints in Rome, on the basis of their experience of 'God's mercy', to reject the pattern of life and society which had previously dominated their existence, and to replace this with a process of *renewal* which would enable them to discern the 'good, pleasing and perfect will of God'. They are no longer to be passive receivers of a system of ethical life and social status imposed upon them by people possessing power and glory, but instead will become a community able to reason, to question and to discern what really is good. Quite clearly the foundation is laid here for a social revolution from below, based on the growth of critical reasoning in the light of the discovery of the will of God. Although the 'pattern of this world' has obvious socio-political implications, it also relates to personal behaviour and the manner in which believers relate to one another within the community of faith. This is evident in the fact that Paul immediately proceeds to say that individuals must not 'think more highly' of themselves than they ought (12:3), but should be 'devoted to one another in love' (12:10). The system of honour and shame is clearly the context for these statements which thus involve an overt challenge to deeply embedded cultural values. There is evidence within Paul's letter that tensions existed both *within and between the tenement and house churches in Rome,* some of which resulted from ethnic differences, others from contrasting social positions, and yet others from disagreements between groups described as the 'weak' and the 'strong' (14:1; 15:1; 16:17). Such differences became the basis for pride and boasting as the endless search for enhanced honour and the avoidance of shame which pervaded the wider society influenced the believing communities, infected their spirituality, and threatened their love and solidarity.

The resonance of Paul's words for Christians in cultures within which the values of honour and shame remain strong today is clear. But what of the developed, technical culture of the Western world, in which such values have long since withered and died, replaced by a situation in which the consumption and ownership of material things becomes almost the only recognized marker of 'progress'? In this situation the call *not to conform to the pattern of this world* has a new reference point, but one which makes it more urgent than ever before. If Paul's vision of a different kind of world, purged of idolatry and shaped by divine grace and justice is to be realized, churches in London and New York, in Manila and Buenos Aires, must discover in the power of the Spirit how to become radically nonconformist, encouraging each other in a process of transformation in line with God's 'good, pleasing and perfect will'.

Second, what form will mission take if it is to reflect the priorities of the apostle to the Gentiles as these are revealed in his correspondence with Rome? Almost at the end of the letter to the Romans, Paul springs a great surprise with the revelation that his desire to visit the imperial capital is not his ultimate goal, since he envisages Rome only as a staging post for a continuing mission to 'the ends of the earth'. His 'longing' to visit believers at the heart of the empire is not an end in itself, but a component in a missionary strategy which has Spain as its ultimate objective. Paul insists: 'I will go to Spain and visit you on the way' (15:28). However, as if one surprise were not enough, he now springs another, announcing that before these extraordinary plans can be realized he must return to Jerusalem 'in the service of the Lord's people there' (15:25). The form of this 'service' involved the delivery of the Gentile 'collection' for the poor of the Jewish church, an act which would fulfil Paul's commitment 'to remember the poor' in Jerusalem (Gal. 2:10). The Pauline vision thus extends to both ends of the

Mediterranean, east and west, and embraces fellow believers in the crucified Messiah at both extremes of the ethnic and religious divide between Jews and Gentiles. On the one hand, his burning ambition is to reach the terra incognita, the virgin territory of Spain, with the message of the gospel, so that where Rome is extending its hegemony by force of arms, the saving and liberating message of God's salvation may be made known. And yet Paul clearly understands that his mission to the 'regions beyond' will only be credible if it is accompanied by concrete evidence that the gospel really can heal a broken world and unite peoples from all nations. Paul's previous missionary work will not be complete if it lacks the fruits of peace, reconciliation and justice, all outcomes of which the Roman Empire boasted, but had so manifestly failed to deliver. The 'collection' therefore involved an act of economic sharing within the body of Christ, extending the radical communalism which the first church in Jerusalem had so strikingly displayed to an international scale and providing concrete evidence of the truth of Paul's proclamation.

This remarkable, empire-wide missionary vision of Paul in the epistle to the Romans has not been recognized in the received traditions of interpretation as being significant in relation to the *purpose and meaning of the letter*.[32] Not the least

---

32. Andrew Walls has shown how specific texts from Romans had massive influence on the nineteenth-century missionary movement, chapter one being frequently discussed, while the number of missionary sermons based on Romans 10:14ff. is 'beyond calculation'. He quotes F. F. Bruce as saying that 'There is no telling what may happen when people begin to read the Epistle to the Romans' since spiritual movements of world-historical significance have emerged as 'very ordinary people' have been grasped by Paul's message. In a century

of the merits of Robert Jewett's recent commentary is that it reads the entire letter from this perspective, seeing the goal of mission in Spain, and the part which Paul clearly hopes the churches in Rome will play in this, as 'crucial for understanding the letter as a whole'.[33] Jewett's discussion of the context of Spain in this period is fascinating and demonstrates how the bulk of the letter, including the central chapters 9 – 11, provide the foundation for Paul's conviction that the Spaniards, 'who are treated as shameful Barbarians', will join every other nation in finding their freedom and hope in Jesus Christ. The ethical challenge which the letter presents to the tenement and house churches in Rome, calling them to live together in love as they follow the way of Christ, is related to this central missiological purpose, because such unity is the precondition for their participation 'in a credible manner in the mission to extend the gospel to the end of the known world'.[34]

The letter to the Romans is thus not only an *urban* document but, to a degree rarely recognized, is crucial to the understanding of *mission* in the New Testament. In the present context discussed earlier in this book, marked by both economic globalization and the emergence of World Christianity, we need fresh and deeper biblical foundations for mission than those which have rested on the use of isolated biblical texts, no matter how cherished and significant these may have been.

---

characterized by the emergence of both globalization and World Christianity we may surely anticipate new and transformative readings of Paul's greatest letter. Andrew Walls, 'Romans One and the Modern Missionary Movement', in *The Missionary Movement in Christian History: Studies in the Transmission of Faith* (Edinburgh: T&T Clark, 1996), pp. 55–67.

33. Jewett, *Romans*, p. 91.

34. Ibid., p. 88.

The letter to the Romans, with its profound challenge to the existing order, its summons to unity, love and mutual respect among peoples from different nations and social backgrounds who confess the crucified Jesus as Messiah and Lord, and its great vision of a world redeemed and transformed, may be about to play a critically important role in the Christian mission in the twenty-first century.[35]

---

35. It is worth noticing that there has been a remarkable recent surge of interest in Paul, particularly in the letter to the Romans, among European philosophers. The catalyst for this is to be found in Stanislas Breton's *A Radical Philosophy of Saint Paul* (New York: Columbia University Press, 2011). Breton was a radical Catholic thinker whose work has triggered a whole series of studies from secular, post-Communist philosophers in search of a new foundation for the vision of a just and transformed world. See Giorgio Agamben, *The Time That Remains: A Commentary on the Letter to the Romans* (Stanford: Stanford University Press, 2005); Alain Badiou, *Saint Paul: The Foundation of Universalism* (Stanford: Stanford University Press, 2003), and various works of Slavoj Žižek. The last-mentioned author enters into dialogue with Christian theologians in John Milbank, Slavoj Žižek and Creston Davis, *Paul's New Moment: Continental Philosophy and the Future of Christian Theology* (Grand Rapids: Brazos Press, 2010). To my knowledge, none of these radical, leftist thinkers have become Christians, but they recognize that the original foundation of the vision of a just and equal world is to be located in Paul's writings. As Žižek puts it, 'We need [a community along the lines of the original Christian community, a community of outcasts] today . . . This is why I and many other leftist philosophers . . . are so interested in rereading, rehabilitating, and reappropriating the legacy of Paul', Slavoj Žižek, 'A meditation on Michaelangelo's *Christ on the Cross*', in Milbank, Žižek and Davis, *Paul's New Moment*, p. 181.

Finally, how does the revelation of the being of God in the letter to the Romans challenge Christian communities in the context of the globalized world of today? Paul's vision is profoundly theocentric; his letter opens with a reference to 'the gospel of God' (1:1), and it ends with a benediction to 'the only wise God' (16:27). In between he wrestles with the mystery of the outworking of the divine purpose in the tangled web of human history, concluding with the acknowledgement that the wisdom and knowledge of God is 'unsearchable' and 'his paths beyond tracing out' (11:33–36). It is as though, having attempted to solve the riddle of the apparent failure of the promises given to biblical Israel, Paul concludes that, while God's intention to have mercy on all peoples remains inviolate (11:32), the pathway to that goal is hidden from human perception, leaving us to walk by faith in the God from whom and through whom and for whom 'are all things' (11:36). In the face of the idolatry and blasphemy propagated by the imperial system in Rome, backed up by the threat of the exclusion of dissenters and the use of lethal force to suppress them, only such a vision of the redeeming, liberating God could sustain faith and keep alive the hope of a different kind of world. What was true then remains true today, so that perhaps the first priority for the church confronting the challenge of globalization, is the recovery of this biblical understanding of God.

But perhaps the statement we most need to attend to is Paul's instruction to believers in the imperial city to consider 'the *kindness and sternness of* God' (11:22). When Paul penned the letter to Rome, Israel was the object of the divine sternness as the result of her failure to fulfil the purpose of her calling in the *missio Dei*. However, Paul argues that this failure has proved to be the means by which the nations have been spiritually enriched and have themselves discovered the divine kindness (11:12). Yet their experience, like that of Israel, remains conditional on their *continuing 'in his kindness'* (11:22). There is a close parallel to this statement in Colossians where those previously 'enemies of God' are promised that they will appear before him 'without blemish and free from accusation – *if you continue in your faith . . .* ' (Col. 1:21–22). Clearly, 'faith' is understood here in a way that cannot mean mere doctrinal certainty, but rather *a trusting fellowship with and obedience to the God whose very essence has been shown to be love and kindness.* For Paul therefore, the greatest threat to the believing community was not located in differences of opinion concerning theology, but rather in *the loss of contact with the God of kindness and mercy, a loss which would lead inexorably to the return of the human pride and arrogance which the revelation of God in the gospel had destroyed.*

This summons to reflect the divine kindness, appearing at the heart of an extended discussion of God's sovereignty and election, is crucial for the integrity and authenticity of mission. It suggests that there is a fluidity, an openness, in the ebb and flow of grace, and it presents us with a sobering reminder that the 'sternness', or holy judgment, of God is as much an expression of his love as is his kindness, or mercy. For believers in ancient Rome this would have come as a reminder that their new status in Christ must not be abused to feed the pride which lurked in the quest for superior honour, and that any failure to reflect the nature of the God of kindness, would result in their fall.

What might this text mean for us two thousand years later in the light of the experience of the collapse of Christendom? Must we not recognize in this historical 'fall', and the rise of a secular culture which has been driven by the quest for human happiness, the *sternness* of God? As long ago as 1883 the commentator Frédérik Godet commented on the condition of

Western Christendom in the light of this text in remarkably perceptive language:

> It is but too clear to anyone who has eyes to see, that our Gentile Christendom has now reached the point here foreseen by St. Paul. In its pride it tramples under foot the very notion of that grace which has made it what it is. It moves on, therefore, to a judgement of rejection like that of Israel, but which shall not have to soften it a promise like that which accompanied the fall of the Jews.[36]

Nonetheless, Paul concludes this passage with the claim that 'God has bound everyone over to disobedience *so that he may have mercy on them all*' (11:32). In the era of economic globalization, with market forces dominant everywhere, a church drawn from every nation, tribe and language is gifted the opportunity to reflect the divine kindness, so becoming a sign to the world of God's grace and mercy and fulfilling the Pauline dream that 'all nations might believe and obey' the 'only wise God' to whom glory is due 'through Jesus Christ' (16:26).

---

36. Quoted in Jewett, *Romans*, p. 691. The original source is Frédéric Godet, *Commentary on St Paul's Epistle to the Romans* (Grand Rapids: Kregel, 1977 [1883]), p. 408.

Conclusion: witness to – and in – the kindness of God

At the beginning of this book I described the context in Nigeria which gave birth to the four chapters which make up its first section and led to the focus on mission in a deeply *troubled world*. I want to return to that particular situation in order to describe some of the conversations which took place in Jos and resulted, as I had hoped and prayed they would, in my own spiritual enrichment and enlarged understanding. The stories I am about to tell provide dramatic examples of the struggles of Christians in different parts of the great continent of Africa, first, to recognize their own compromises with patterns of belief and action inconsistent with the gospel and, second, to rediscover the authentic message of Christ and allow it to become the 'script' which would reshape their lives and their communities.

These narratives will illustrate how the kind of conflicting readings of the Bible which we have noticed occurring throughout the history of the Christian movement are still surfacing today. And yet, the experiences recorded here are important, above all, because they bear witness to the continuing discovery of that 'other Voice', heard amid tragedy, suffering and oppression, calling those it addresses to 'hope against hope' and to follow the way of Jesus Christ. These are narratives that, alas, bear witness to apostasy, syncretism and tragic ethical failures, but they tell too of a host of brave people who, awakened to reality by that 'other Voice', have joined battle in resistance to deeply engrained structural evils, have shown mercy and love toward the suffering and oppressed, and have found previously unknown resources to love each other across barriers which had previously appeared to be impenetrable.

Renouncing the idols, confessing the faith

The conference in Jos attracted theological teachers from across Nigeria and was addressed by a number of speakers from other parts of the continent of Africa. Among these speakers was Johan Botha, a minister of the Uniting Reformed Church in Southern Africa (URCSA) and a man whose own family has a distinguished history of missionary service in the central belt of Nigeria. In his presentations to the conference, and in private conversations, he shared something of the spiritual and theological journey he and his compatriots in South Africa had travelled both during and after the apartheid era in that country.

The political doctrine of apartheid had its roots in the policies and teaching of the Dutch Reformed Church in South Africa as far back as the middle of the nineteenth century, when the separation of Christians into congregations segregated on the basis of race and colour began to be practiced. In 1857 this church, having previously resisted attempts to implement racial segregation, declaring such a policy to be inconsistent with Scripture, now yielded to growing demands from its core constituency and permitted white congregations to celebrate the Lord's Supper apart from their black brothers and sisters. This fateful decision set in motion a process which was to lead, first, to racially segregated churches, and eventually to the application of this principle to the wider social and political spheres. However, as John de Gruchy has pointed out, British colonial policy in South Africa was also based on the premise of 'the separation of the white settler community from the black indigenous communities' and in the aftermath of the Anglo-Boer War, the British authorities attempted 'to reconcile two settler communities in a united white nation'.[1] The indigenous, black populations were excluded by the constitution of the Union of South Africa in 1910 and three years later a law was passed which reserved more than 85% of the land area of South Africa for white ownership and control, leaving the disenfranchized native populations dependent on whatever largesse the ruling class might be disposed to make. As tensions inevitably increased, so the conviction grew among the Afrikaans population that people from different races and of different skin colour, not only belonged in different churches, but that it would serve 'the best interests of all races if they developed separately and independently not only in the church, but in society as well'.[2] By 1948, the growth of Afrikaner nationalism resulted in the achievement of political power by people who were ideologically committed to a policy of 'separate development', and the

---

1. John W. de Gruchy, *Reconciliation. Restoring Justice* (London: SCM Press, 2002), p. 31.

2. Johan Botha and Piet Naude, *Good News to Confess: The Belhar Confession and the Road of Acceptance* (Wellington SA: Bible Media, 2011), p. 45. The outline of developments within the Dutch Reformed communities in this and following paragraphs is largely dependent upon this source.

hegemony of the white population became shaped 'by Afrikaner interests and supported by a more refined ideology of racial superiority, namely apartheid'.[3] Apartheid as a political doctrine was now enforced by a whole series of draconian laws which made possible a massive exercise of social engineering involving the forced relocation of hundreds of thousands of people. Botha describes the consequences:

> Areas where different races had lived together for years were declared undesirable and had to be evacuated by all but one group. Consequently, thousands of people were forced to sell their properties at huge losses and move elsewhere, leaving them with only intense homesickness and longing for how things once were. Apartheid laws broke the hearts of many people, many were driven into poverty, and some lost all hope and their taste for life. Some committed suicide; in others the bitterness and hatred towards their fellow countrymen grew, and many lost their faith in God.[4]

While, as we have seen, the Dutch Reformed Church was complicit in these developments and justified them on the basis of its revised reading of the Bible, many members of the wider Reformed tradition opposed segregation and the fundamentally racist attitudes which accompanied it. Within the Dutch Reformed Mission Church (DRMC), whose very name indicates a history of witness and service within black African communities, the policy was resisted from the beginning. A former moderator of this church wrote in 1960 that while apartheid might succeed in segregating black and white, 'we are sharpening the blade that may pierce our own

---

3. De Gruchy, *Reconciliation*, p. 32.

4. Ibid., p. 46.

heart'. A decade later this prophecy began to be fulfilled as the sufferings of the black population gave birth to growing resistance, while those holding power defended manifestly unjust structures with ever greater violence and brutality.

Piet Naude describes an experience which took place while he was attending a meeting of the South African Council of Churches in Johannesburg in 1985, during which participants were asked to attend the memorial service for five African boys killed by booby-trapped grenades, which, it was suspected, the security forces had planted. The area around the church was devastated and the streets filled with heavily armed military personnel. Inside the church children with clenched fists sang a song in their vernacular language which brought a rebuke from an elderly lady. Sitting down beside the pastor of an African Independent Church, Naude enquired about the song and, after initial resistance to revealing is content, the pastor said, 'The children sang, "the boers are dogs" and the sister said one should not sing about others in that manner'. Naude writes:

> I froze. Shortly afterwards, when the children sang 'When he cometh, when he cometh, to make up his jewels', I was so overcome with emotion that I could not join them. I cried because I was struck by the immensity of the gulf that existed between the worlds in which our children lived – within our one, shared motherland.[5]

By this time the pressures on white, Afrikaans-speaking Christians were not only internal, arising from experiences like the one just described, but external, as the voices of

---

5. Ibid., p. 81. The reference to a 'shared motherland' seems rather incongruous in the light of the fact that the original owners of the land now had access to only 15% of it.

protest and condemnation increased in number and volume around the world. In August 1982, a meeting of the World Alliance of Reformed Churches held in Ottawa, Canada, agreed that the situation in South Africa constituted a *status confessionis*, a formal declaration that the truth and credibility of the gospel itself was being placed in jeopardy by the way in which the Bible was being used to justify the apartheid system. When this decision was reported to the assembly of the Dutch Reformed Mission Church a few weeks later, it led to a significant development in which this church accepted the Ottawa verdict and repudiated apartheid as a 'secular gospel' which ran completely counter to the message of reconciliation in the Bible. The 'other Voice' was being heard once again, as can be seen in the words of a leading theologian who spoke during the DRMC assembly:

> I now have reached a place where I understand and experience the rules of apartheid as applied in my life, both by state and church, as the consequence of viewpoints and convictions *that are in direct opposition to the way in which I understand the gospel of Jesus Christ.*[6]

The speaker was Professor Gustav Bam, who went on to draw a comparison between the context of Christians in apartheid South Africa and those of the early church in the Roman Empire and of the 'Confessing Church' in Germany during the Nazi period. In such times, he said, faith urgently needed confession in contextual language which related precisely to the particular threat which the reigning ideology presented to the integrity of the gospel of Jesus Christ. The language of the Barmen Declaration of 1934 had combined

---

6. Ibid., p. 56, emphasis added.

the confession of unequivocal faithfulness to the gospel with a clear reference to the specific historical context in which Christians then found themselves. On the one hand, it confessed that Christ is 'the one Word whom we have to hear' while explicitly repudiating the 'false doctrine' that the church might add 'other events, powers, historic figures and truths as God's revelation'. According to Bam, the situation in South Africa was now so grave and perilous that it demanded a similar act of confession in which the supreme authority of Christ would be proclaimed over and against the particular forms of idolatry then regnant in South Africa. These idols, whether in the form of social structures or of ideological systems, needed to be named and rejected.

This moving and unexpected plea was unanimously accepted and work began on drafting a confession of faith for a church threatened by a highly contextual form of heresy. Four years later, in September 1982, after a process of drafting and redrafting involving detailed discussions within DRMC congregations and presbyteries, the Belhar Confession was approved.[7] It explicitly rejected 'the unevangelical convictions and theology on which apartheid was based', while affirming three crucial issues for the life of the faithful church in such a situation: 'lived and visible unity, true reconciliation, and compassionate justice.'[8] We will return to this document later, but its acceptance as a new confessional statement, notwithstanding strong opposition to it from within the Dutch Reformed Church itself, was a moment of great significance for Christians within the Reformed tradition. Johan Botha recalled how the sense of renewed joy and hope when the

---

7. Belhar being the town in which the DRMC assembly which adopted the Confession met.

8. De Gruchy, *Reconciliation*, p. 75.

confession was accepted brought to mind the thanksgiving of the psalmist when 'the LORD restored the fortunes of Zion' and enabled a despairing and broken people to say: 'The LORD has done great things for us' (Ps. 126:1–3).

The cries of the oppressed

At the very point at which a minority of Afrikaans-speaking Christians within the white population of South Africa were recognizing and confessing their complicity in apartheid, believers on the other side of the 'dividing wall' created by this cruel and dehumanizing system were raising their voices in angry protests against the injustices they suffered. The famous *Kairos Document* appeared in September 1985, signed by 156 people, representing no less than twenty South African Christian denominations. This statement, which was subtitled *Challenge to the Church: A Theological Comment on the Political Crisis in South Africa*, was a passionate and angry reflection, produced within the township of Soweto, Johannesburg, under the pressure of a rapidly deteriorating situation. Those who drafted the document described it as 'an attempt by concerned Christians in South Africa to reflect on the situation of death in our country'. They pointed out that growing numbers of people were indeed dying as the crisis intensified and 'the apartheid army moved into the townships to rule by the barrel of the gun'.[9] The opening words reflect very clearly the almost desperate sense of urgency felt by its compilers:

---

9. *Challenge to the Church: A Theological Comment on the Political Crisis in South Africa – The Kairos Document, 1985,* <http://www.sahistory.org.za/archive/challenge-church-theological-comment-political-crisis-south-africa-kairos-document-1985> (accessed 20 September 2012).

The time has come. The moment of truth has arrived. South Africa has been plunged into a crisis that is shaking the foundations and there is every indication that the crisis has only just begun and that it will deepen and become even more threatening . . . It is the KAIROS moment of truth not only for apartheid but also for the church.

However, what the crisis revealed concerning the church in South Africa was precisely its *division*; Christians were to be found on both sides of the dividing wall created by apartheid, some defending the system, while others saw it as an abomination, so that 'oppressor and oppressed claim loyalty to the same church'. What is more, both sides appealed to the authority of the Bible, prompting the question whether 'the Bible can be used for any purpose at all?' By now we are familiar with this issue which, as we have seen in earlier chapters, has repeatedly arisen throughout Christian history. The response of the authors of the *Kairos Document* involved subjecting different types of theology to a sharply critical analysis. What they described as 'State Theology' involved the co-option of Christianity in support and defence of an unjust and blatantly racist system, resulting in the radical *subversion* of the gospel of Jesus Christ. For example, the South African constitution used god-language in its preamble, professing 'humble submission to Almighty God' who 'gathered our forebears together from many lands and gave them this their own'. The liberating God of the Bible was here transformed into the guarantor of a state which disenfranchized the majority of its population, while gifting land and economic and political power to an elect minority. The *Kairos Document* denounced this use of 'God's holy name' as an act of *blasphemy* involving the creation of an idol designed to justify an unjust and oppressive state. 'Here is a god who exalts the proud and humbles the poor – the very opposite of the God of the Bible who "scatters the proud of heart, pulls down the mighty from their thrones and exalts the humble" (Lk. 1:51–52).'

The second type of theology to be critically evaluated within the *Kairos Document* is what the authors classify as 'Church Theology', by which is meant the theology underlying the official, published statements of the leaders of mainline, white denominations. It is acknowledged that such statements are cautiously critical of apartheid, but they are subjected to strong criticism on account of the fact that their central response to the situation is always to talk in terms of the need for *reconciliation*. This leads into a passage which, while it was the most controversial in the entire document and sparked much debate, has considerable significance in relation to precisely the contexts of social division and escalating violence with which this present book has been centrally concerned. Church Theology, according to those who drafted the *Kairos Document*, turned the biblical theme of reconciliation into an 'absolute principle' and failed to realize that its simplistic application to a context like that in apartheid South Africa ignored fundamentally important elements in that situation.[10]

There are conflicts where one side is a fully armed and violent oppressor while the other side is defenceless and oppressed.

---

10. John de Gruchy comments on the 'heated controversy' which erupted 'around the meaning of reconciliation' as repressive measures were taken by the government against those associated with the *Kairos Document*. 'Clearly there was hesitation about the ideological abuse of such a key doctrine of the Christian faith, whether by those who used it in defence of their supposed neutrality, or those who rejected it as counter-productive to the struggle', De Gruchy, *Reconciliation*, p. 36.

There are conflicts that can only be described as the struggle between justice and injustice, good and evil, God and the devil. To speak of reconciling these two is not only a mistaken application of the Christian idea of reconciliation, it is a total betrayal of all that the Christian faith has ever meant. Nowhere in the Bible or in Christian tradition has it ever been suggested that we ought to try to reconcile good and evil, God and the devil. We are supposed to do away with evil, injustice, oppression and sin – not to come to terms with it.

While the desperate situation which gave birth to this document must never be forgotten, and while the statement that 'reconciliation' is cheapened when it becomes a slogan which disguises hard reality is justified, the claim made here, that the line between good and evil, and God and the devil, can be drawn with such absolute clarity and certainty is alarming. We have seen many situations, both historically and in recent global politics, in which such claims have been made and without fail they result in the demonizing of one's enemies and a terrifying confidence in the righteousness of one's own cause. When the document goes on to state that reconciliation in South Africa is impossible *without justice and repentance* it is surely on firmer ground and moves toward a reinstatement of a biblical theme which, contrary to the quotation above, must remain of fundamental importance in precisely such situations. In challenging this section of the statement we take up the invitation of its authors to 'develop the themes' they presented 'or to criticize them and return to the Bible'.

The discussion of 'Church Theology' extends across many pages and includes a critique of one-sided condemnations of violence in official church statements in which acts of resistance to tyranny are always condemned, while 'the structural, institutional and unrepentant violence of the State' is treated as legitimate and never confronted in the name of Christ. Consequently, the phrase 'violence in the townships' comes to mean 'what the young people are doing and not what the police are doing or what apartheid in general is doing to people'. This section of the document raises issues that remain of fundamental importance to contexts in which violence is escalating, as in the Middle Belt of Nigeria, and indeed, throughout an increasingly 'troubled world'.

The final theological category is 'Prophetic Theology' which moves beyond the distortions and limitations of the currently dominant ways of doing theology and is unambiguously affirmed as the clear and urgent priority. Such theology involves careful social analysis as the foundation for a biblical critique of oppression and injustice, but interestingly, this section closes with an emphasis on *hope*. God is at work turning hopeless situations around so that his kingdom may come, and this deep conviction results in the belief 'that goodness and justice and love will triumph in the end and that tyranny and oppression cannot last forever'. What is more, the biblical message of hope can release the oppressors from their false hopes and terrible fears; they also 'need something to hope for'. The document closes with a ringing call to the church to be the church; her confessions of faith must be 're-shaped to be more fully consistent with a prophetic faith related to the KAIROS that God is offering us today'. The repentance which is required to enter the kingdom of God must be given concrete form in the confession of 'our share in the guilt for the suffering and oppression in our country'. The evils renounced in Christian baptism 'must be named', while the unity shared at the Lord's Table needs to be expressed as a solidarity in the struggle for God's peace in South Africa.

While the *Kairos Document* may now be treated as a record of historical events, much of what it says has continuing relevance in the world we have described in this present book. Indeed, in this 'troubled world', in which scholars now describe the growth of a 'military urbanism' as geopolitical contests trigger 'violent conflicts' in contemporary cities, the anguished search in this document for faithful theological and ethical responses to violence can and should be an important resource for Christians who seek to walk the way of Jesus Christ in the twenty-first century.[11]

What of the evangelicals?

In the year following the issuing of the *Kairos Document* another meeting of black Christian leaders took place in Soweto, Johannesburg, at which 132 people, who identified themselves as 'concerned evangelicals', gathered to discuss the South African crisis. During their initial meeting the security forces stormed into the adjacent school and children were seen breaking window panes in order to escape. The violence escalated and triggered the inevitable response of stone-throwing and attempts to set vehicles on fire. Those who had met together asked themselves: 'What was our

---

11. See Stephen Graham, *Cities Under Siege: The New Military Urbanism* (London: Verso, 2010), for a comprehensive discussion of the militarization of urban spaces in which new, military-style command and control systems are being created 'to support "zero tolerance" policing and urban surveillance practices designed to exclude failed consumers or undesirable persons from the new enclaves of urban consumption and leisure', p. 23.

response supposed to be in this situation as evangelical Christians in South Africa?'[12]

By this time the *Kairos Document* had been widely circulated but the evangelicals decided to produce their own response to the crisis in order to undertake a critical review of their own, distinctive theology. 'We felt', they wrote, 'that although our perception of the gospel helped us to be what we are, saved by the blood of the Lord Jesus Christ . . . our theology nevertheless was inadequate to address the crisis we were facing.'[13] In this case the theology concerned was largely imported, a legacy of the Western missionary movement. As the group met over a period of months, they reached the conclusion that the missionary theology they had received, and which had been presented as a culture-free version of the gospel, was in fact 'influenced by American and European missionaries with political, social and class interests which were contrary or even hostile to both the spiritual and social needs of our people in this country'. This scathing criticism of missionary theology surfaces repeatedly in the statement which the group issued in July 1986, under the title *Evangelical Witness in South Africa: South African Evangelicals Critique Their Own Theology and Practice*. The document observes that 'some enthusiastic missionary evangelists' from the West had refused to challenge the apartheid system on the grounds that this would 'jeopardise their ministry' and result in their deportation. Non-interference in local politics was essential, so it was argued, for the sake of the gospel. The rejoinder is uncompromising: 'It is for this reason that people are rejecting

---

12. *Evangelical Witness in South Africa: South African Evangelicals Critique Their Own Theology and Practice* (Oxford: Regnum Books, 1986), p. 9.

13. Ibid., p. 10.

the gospel in their struggles for liberation because of the collaboration of most western pioneers of the gospel with oppressive systems in the two-thirds world (Third World).'[14]

The critique becomes sharper still in a discussion of the social and cultural conditioning which results in different people reading 'the same text' yet discerning opposite meanings within it. Yet again we encounter here a situation in which people reading the Bible reach conflicting conclusions, in this case with regard to imperialism and colonialism. Black Evangelicals in Soweto observed that Western Christians regard 'the wave of colonization as a victory for the missionary enterprise and the spread of what they called Christian civilization'. White missionaries from the developed West invariably failed to acknowledge the brutalization of native peoples under colonialism, treating the advance of the West as no more and no less than a providential opening for Christianization. European and American Evangelicals appeared to be 'blind to western domination and exploitation of the peoples of the Third World', focused as they were on the primary task of 'winning souls', regardless of the 'pain and suffering people are going through'. Colonialist attitudes persisted where missionaries treated black Africans as the 'mission field', while regarding themselves as the bearers of truth and civilization. 'They still see Africa as a "dark" continent which needs the gospel when there are more lapsed Christians or non-Christians in Europe and in white South Africa.'[15]

The anger so clearly reflected in these statements needs to be understood in relation to the context we have already described, but we must also recognize the underlying motives

14. Ibid., p. 23.
15. Ibid., p. 25.

which compelled those who drafted the document to speak with such directness and honesty. It is very clear that these African Evangelicals had realized that the message of the gospel in the form in which they had been taught to preach it was failing to connect with the reality of the lives of young people in the townships. A dualistic theology which placed social and political action off limits for the true Christian had rendered believers powerless and speechless with regard to the life-and-death issues which they confronted daily in apartheid South Africa. Consequently, a generation gap was opening up as the message of salvation increasingly lost critical contact with the host culture. The received methodologies of proclamation through evangelistic campaigns and 'crusades' were increasingly redundant; preaching was being 'swallowed up by the cries of the poor and oppressed' and these voices were now so loud and insistent as to drown out Christian proclamation. This situation made it imperative to broaden the evangelical understanding of mission and evangelism because, without this, Christian ministry 'is doomed in this country'. The language of the 'Kairos moment' is absent from this document, but the reality is present everywhere:

> Faced with this trouble-torn country, faced with the war between the apartheid regime and the oppressed masses, faced with the ideological conflicts which are tearing our communities apart, and confronted with the possibility of a revolution, *our response and choices will determine the future of Christian faith in this country.*[16]

This document, produced by Christians who clearly wished to retain an identity as 'evangelicals', poses some searching

---

16. Ibid., p. 17, emphasis added.

and disturbing questions for their brothers and sisters in the Western world, especially those associated with the missionary movement. While we must recognize that the anger which surfaces here is explained by the immediate context, in which what amounted to an army of occupation frequently appeared out of control within black townships, and while the critique of missions and missionaries may not be taken as an accurate account of the work of all white missionaries, or of the missionary movement as a whole, nonetheless, the critical analysis of Western missionary theology and practice within this document poses serious questions, many of which still remain unaddressed among many evangelicals in Europe and the United States. Indeed, the very term 'evangelical' has, since the 1980s, become increasingly devalued by its association with a form of fundamentalist religion which remains immensely powerful and deploys precisely the kind of arguments in defence of Western civilization which are so decisively repudiated in this document. Although *Evangelical Witness in South Africa* is a highly contextual statement, the central themes it articulated have been repeated by Christians in many other similar situations across the Global South, and in the world we have tried to describe in this book the time is long past for the churches of the Western world to hear these cries and respond with repentance, reformation and a new humility.

Return to Belhar

The Belhar Confession which we discussed at the beginning of this chapter, was adopted within the Dutch Reformed Mission Church in 1982, and within four years of that event both the statements which we have just discussed had emerged from the other side of the 'dividing wall' created by apartheid.

In all three of these documents, which are different in many respects, there is an explicit repudiation of apartheid, a clarion call for justice and repentance, and a demand for the church to recover the fullness of the gospel and to model the way of Christ within its own life. Whether there was dialogue between these groups across the divides created by race, language and theological traditions, I do not know, but I am struck by the manner in which the words of the Belhar Confession offer a basis for unity in love, not only for separated Christians in South Africa, but across the whole continent, especially in situations of tension, division and social injustice. Indeed, the thrust of this confessional statement, forged out of deep pain and anguish, seems to me to provide such rich insights into the very core of Christian identity that it needs to be shared beyond the Reformed constituency in South Africa which brought it to birth. Out of the terrible divisions and sufferings of the different communities of this land came a confession which may prove a blessing to Christian believers elsewhere, both within Africa and far beyond it. In fact, in the new, post-apartheid situation in South Africa itself, in which one of the key players in the drafting of the *Kairos Document* now writes about the loss of hope and the need to stress personal freedom and a 'radical spirituality' without which social activism will lack an adequate foundation, the Belhar Confession can be received as one of God's best gifts from this tumultuous period.[17]

---

17. See Albert Nolan, *Hope in an Age of Despair* (New York: Orbis Books, 2009). Nolan was a central figure in the struggle against apartheid. He writes: 'In South Africa an enormous amount of hope was generated by the struggle itself and by its success in dismantling apartheid, by the negotiated settlement, by a relatively peaceful transition to democracy, by our new constitution, and by

It is not possible to reproduce the entire confession and the important letter which accompanied it, but I want to quote the following passages as examples of the originality and contextual relevance of this statement in our 'troubled world' today.

After a brief first section confessing faith in the triune God, Belhar moves immediately to the nature of the church:

> We believe in one, holy, universal Christian Church, the communion of saints called from the entire human family.
>
> We believe that Christ's work of reconciliation is made manifest in the church as the community of believers who have been reconciled with God and with one another; [. . .]
>
> that this unity must become visible so that the world may believe that separation, enmity and hatred between people and groups is sin which Christ has already conquered, and accordingly that anything which threatens this unity may have no place in the church and must be resisted; [. . .]
>
> that this unity can be established only in freedom and not under constraint; that the variety of spiritual gifts, opportunities, backgrounds, convictions, as well as the diversity of languages and cultures, are by virtue of the reconciliation in Christ, opportunities for mutual service and enrichment within the one people of God; [. . .]
>
> Therefore, we reject any doctrine
>
> Which absolutises either natural diversity or the sinful separation of people in such a way that this absolutisation

---

the charismatic leadership of Mandela. But since then our hopes have been gradually eroded, and today the general mood can only be described as disillusionment and despair', p. 5.

hinders or breaks the visible unity of the church, or even leads
to the establishment of a separate church formation; [. . .]

Which explicitly or implicitly maintains that descent or any
other human or social factor should be a consideration in
determining membership of the church.

The third section is concerned with the gospel and its
credibility:

We believe that God has entrusted the church with the
message of reconciliation in and through Jesus Christ; that
the church is called to be the salt of the earth and the light
of the world and that the church is called blessed because it
is a peacemaker, that the church is witness both by word
and by deed to the new heaven and the new earth in which
righteousness dwells; [. . .]

that the credibility of this message is seriously affected and its
beneficial work obstructed when it is proclaimed in a land that
professes to be Christian, but in which the enforced separation
of people on a racial basis promotes and perpetuates alienation,
hatred and enmity; that any teaching which attempts to
legitimate such forced separation by appeal to the gospel,
and is not prepared to venture on the road of obedience and
reconciliation, but rather, out of prejudice, fear, selfishness and
unbelief, denies in advance the reconciling power of the gospel,
must be considered ideology and false doctrine. [. . .]

The fourth section confesses God's promise of peace and
justice and its implications for the life of the church:

We believe that God has revealed Godself as the One who
wishes to bring about justice and true peace on the earth; that

in a world full of injustice and enmity God is in a special way
the God of the destitute, the poor and the wronged and that
God calls the church to follow in this; that God brings justice to
the oppressed and gives bread to the hungry; that God frees the
prisoner and restores sight to the blind; that God supports the
downtrodden, protects the strangers, helps orphans and
widows and blocks the path of the ungodly; that for God pure
and undefiled religion is to visit the orphans and widows in
their suffering; that God wishes to teach the people of God to
do what is good and to seek the right;

That the church must therefore stand by people in any form
of suffering and need, which implies, among other things, that
the church must witness against any form of injustice, so that
justice may roll down like waters, and righteousness like an
ever-flowing stream;

That the church belonging to God, should stand where God
stands, namely against injustice and with the wronged; that
in following Christ the church must witness against all the
powerful and privileged who selfishly seek their own interests
and thus control and harm others.

Therefore, we reject any ideology which would legitimate
forms of injustice and any doctrine which is unwilling to resist
such an ideology in the name of the gospel.

The final section is an affirmation of faith and a renewed
commitment to obedience:

We believe that, in obedience to Jesus Christ, its only Head,
the church is called to confess and to do all these things, even
though authorities and human laws might forbid them and
punishment and suffering be the consequence.

Jesus is Lord.

To the one and only God, Father, Son and Holy Spirit, be the honour and the glory for ever and ever.[18]

On the fault line between Christianity and Islam

If the meeting with Johan Botha at the conference in Jos, Nigeria, was one source of blessing and enrichment for me, another was the opportunity this event gave for renewed fellowship with Professor Danny McCain. The service which this remarkable man has given in mission in Africa constitutes a model of humble, self-sacrificing discipleship which, had it been characteristic of Western and North American mission as a whole, would have completely disarmed the kind of critique we have just noted. Danny McCain is Professor of Biblical Theology in the Department of Religious Studies in the University of Jos, having previously taught at Rivers State University of Science and Technology in Port Harcourt. He has been a prolific teacher and writer and a Christian activist forever pouring out his life in the service of other people. His love for the African church, and for the land of Nigeria, is deep and sincere. When I met with Danny in the quietness of the chapel at the Theological College of Northern Nigeria, he was kind enough to give me a copy of his latest book, *To The Ends of the Earth: Geographical and Cross-Cultural Challenges for Twenty-First Century Christians*. On the flight back to London I read this book with much profit, but was arrested by one particular story within it. Danny McCain, and the

---

18. Botha and Naude, *Good News to Confess*, pp. 19–22. The full text of the Belhar Confession, together with the accompanying letter, can be viewed on the URCSA website, <http://www.vgksa.org.za/Confessions.asp>.